Preface

I really never thought of writing a book on Gandhi. In fact, I hardly ever cared for reading Gandhi seriously. The reason,however, which prompted me to read Gandhi a bit seriously was twofold. The first is purely academic and the second is realistic, i.e., true to the actual state of affairs. The academic reason consists in the fact that so often I heard from many quarters, sometimes from important quarters, that religion and politics should never be mixed together. Doing this kind of mix up sometimes produces worst kind of social evil. On the other hand, a great man like Gandhi I heard saying that politics without religion was like a dead body which polluted society and politics both. Politics devoid of religion was very harmful. I however wondered what made Gandhi say this. It hardly needs mention that the events of our own country for sometime now have made the topic all the more important.It is this curiosity which led me to study of Gandhi's thought. In course of my study I could certainly know the exact sense in which Gandhi wanted religion to be a necessary part of politics, but the more important thing I could gather as a student of philosophy from my studies of Gandhi's thought was that almost all the important concepts – *Satya, ahimsā, satyāgraha* etc. - were formed under this primary impact of his religious convictions which he derived mostly, although not exclusively, from Hinduism.

The second reason came from my son Dr. Rajesh Ranjan Tiwari himself, who has been a student of Philosophy, and is now University Professor and Head of the Dept of Philosophy, T. M.

Bhagalpur University. During his teaching career it is a matter of chance that he was for some time posted by the university administration in the Dept of Gandhian Thought itself to help improve the quality of teaching and research there. This gave him an occasion to see things with his own eyes. During his stay there, he always complained that in spite of several books in the market and libraries, there was an obvious dearth of some such books on Gandhi which thoroughly analysed his key concepts so that one could clearly understand what important features were involved and implied in these concepts which really revolutionised the theory and practice both of the followers of Gandhi. Dr Tiwari really motivated and inspired me to write such a book on Gandhi. With his inspiration and pressure, I decided to read Gandhi thoroughly and finally wrote this book which is in front of you.

Because Gandhi was, as he himself repeatedly said, a thoroughly religious man, therefore my primary aim in the book has been to see the impact that religion with all the prevailing religions has exerted on him in the formation of his various concepts. But before doing that, I have thoroughly analysed the ingredients of each and every Gandhian concept so that its main features must be brought forth before the readers. Moreover I have always been aware that in forming his concept, he has been influenced greatly not only by the different religions, but also by the great writers and thinkers like Tolstoy, Ruskin, Thoreau, C. F. Andrews and several such other thinkers. I have not totally ignored their influences on Gandhi in my book and have made a thorough mention of them wherever it has been necessary.

Whatever I have said above about the internals of the writing of the book, I think, calls for my first and foremost thanks to Dr Rajesh Ranjan Tiwari, who actually motivated and inspired me to write a book on Gandhi of the type I have finally given shape to. Secondly it is Sri Abhishek Jain, the Managing Director of Motilal Banarsidas International, who deserves my hearty thanks, because

THE IMPACT OF RELIGIONS
ON
GANDHI'S THOUGHT

The Impact of Religions
on
Gandhi's Thought

K. N. TIWARI

**MOTILAL BANARSIDASS
INTERNATIONAL
DELHI**

First edition: Delhi, 2023

ISBN : 978-81-19394-86-9

Also available at
MOTILAL BANARSIDASS INTERNATIONAL
H. O. : 41 U.A. Bungalow Road, (Back Lane) Jawahar Nagar, Delhi - 110 007
4261/3 (basement), Ansari Road, Darya Ganj, New Delhi - 110 002
203 Royapettah High Road, Mylapore, Chennai - 600 004
12/1A, 2nd Floor, Bankim Chatterjee Street, Kolkata - 700 073
Stockist : Motilal Books, Ashok Rajpath, Near Kali Mandir, Patna - 800 004

Printed in India
MOTILAL BANARSIDASS INTERNATIONAL

(vii)

the moment a proposal of publishing the above type of book on Gandhi was put before him by me, he readily accepted the same without taking any kind of pleas.

Shanti Sadan   **Kedar Nath Tiwari**
Budhanath
Bhagalpur

Introduction

Gandhi's thought is multi-dimensional. It has at least a religious, a social a political and an economic dimension. All these dimensions of Gandhi's thought have taken some concrete shape in the form of certain concepts such as God, Man, *Satya, Ahimsā, Satyāgraha, Sarvodaya, Swarāj, Swadeshi,* Bread labour, Trusteeship etc. These concepts were formed under various influences from various sides. In the main, the influences were from the side of certain great authors like Thoreau, Tolstoy, Ruskin etc, some of the great books like the *Bhagavad Gitā,* the *Quran,* the *New Testament* of *Bible,* Arnold's *The Light of Asia* and *The Song Celestial,* Carlyle's *Heroes and Hero-worship* etc. and some of the great religions like Hinduism, Jainism, Buddhism, Christianity and Islam. Here in the present work we shall concentrate mainly on the influences exerted by the great religions of the world in the formation of Gandhian concepts.

Apparently, throughout his career, Gandhi seemed to be a politician or a political man. But as Gandhi himself repeatedly asserted, he was basically a religious man with an essentially religious or spiritual goal in mind to achieve. Politics was only a garb through which he wanted to achieve his religious goal. As he himself asserts in this connection, "Most religious men I have met are politicians in disguise; I, however, who wears the guise of a politician, am at heart a religious man."[1] Gandhi further said that he had to be involved in political life with a sense of necessity and compulsion. Politics "encircled the entire life of man" like "the coils of a snake" and he wanted to wrestle with this snake. His countrymen were under political subjugation and were suffering a kind of political tyranny. He wanted liberation of his people from this tyranny. That is why he had put on the garb of a politician. Moreover, politics had become a sphere of immorality, injustice, tyranny and all such evils. He wanted purification of politics. He wanted to introduce religion into politics. Politics without religion was, according to him, like a corpse fit to be burnt. Thus It was religion which led him to politics. He wanted liberation of his people as well as purification of politics. In a way, thus, it was with a purely religious motive that Gandhi adopted politics. His frequently religious attitude towards life that he possessed behind and beneath his apparently political life can be seen through his following straightforward statement also ".....at the back of every word that I have uttered since I have known what public life is, and every act that I have done, there has been a religious consciousness and a downright religious motive."[2] The primacy of religious motive behind Gandhi's all social and political activities can also be seen through some of his statements in which he has accepted in an unqualified manner that his sole motive behind all his activities was nothing but self-realization or the realization of God. It is for this and this alone that he had been working ceaselessly in different roles for several years. He took social service of the poor and the weak to be his chief concern because he had the firm belief that it was only through such services that he could realise God.

Gandhi had his own conception of religion which we shall see in due course, but under this conception he believed that there was no difference between God and human self and that all human beings were at bottom one. Therefore, it was only through the service of human beings, especially of the poor and the downtrodden, that God could be realised. So he was seeking God in the poor and the helpless. His political activity also was motivated mainly by this aim. His chief political activity consisted in liberating his countrymen from the bondage of the British rule, and this also he did with the same motive of the service of the suffering humanity. Because his countrymen where he immediate neighbours, hit took it as his primary duty to work for their liberation. All these points become very clear from his own following statement: "What I want to achieve....., what I have been striving and pinning to achieve this 30 years..... is self-realization, to see God face to face, to attain *Moksha*. I live and move and have my being in pursuit of this goal. All that I do by way of speaking and writing and all my ventures in the political field are directed to this same end."[3] Reasserting his views, Gandhi speaks again in somewhat a different language, "Man's ultimate aim is the realization of God and his activities, social, political, religious have to be guided by the aim of the vision of God. The immediate service of all human beings becomes a necessary part of the endeavour, simply because the only way to find God is to see Him in His creation and be one with it. This can only be done by service of all. I am part and parcel of the whole and I cannot find Him apart from the rest of the humanity. My countrymen are my nearest neighbours. They have become so helpless, so resourceless, so inert that I must concentrate myself on serving them."[4] In a way Gandhi has depicted his whole philosophy of life in the above statement and one can see through it how deeply moral and religious Gandhi's fundamental outlook has been.

Due to his essentially religious bent of mind, Gandhi was very critical of modern civilization which was according to him out and out materialistic in nature. He indicted modern civilisation for its mad pursuit of material wealth and bodily comfort along with a total disregard of moral and religious values. Criticising modern civilization for its total irreligious outlook, Gandhi said, "This civilization is irreligion, and it has taken such a hold on the people in Europe that those who are in it appear to be half mad. They lack physical strength or courage. They keep up their energy by intoxication. They can hardly be happy in solitude......"[5] These remarks indicate how much concerned Gandhi was about the lack of morality and religion in modern civilization. He wanted to introduce morality and religion in every sphere of life so that men could be men in the real sense of the term. He did not take material progress as a sign of the real progress of man. He was guided in his thought and action by the Hindu, Jain and Buddhist ideals of non-possession (*aparigrah*) and took moral and spiritual uplift of man as the real sign of his progress. He referred explicitly to this teaching of the various religions that we should not be very much engrossed in worldly materials. We should rather set a limit to our worldly ambitions and be engaged in moral and spiritual pursuits. Moral progress, he said, stands in an inverse ratio to material progress.

The above clearly shows that Gandhi wanted man to lead a thoroughly moral and religious life. He wanted to introduce religion in every sphere of life. However, his conception of religion was very broad and he did not mean by it any kind of sectarian belief. He said that he believed in a religion which underlined all religions. No historical religion, according to him, could claim exclusive or absolute truth. Nevertheless, he liked Hinduism because it did not believe in exclusivism. According to Hinduism all religious express the same truth in their own different ways. Thus although Gandhi had deep regard for all the religions of the world, he always preferred to remain a Hindu. He was a Hindu by birth and he liked to remain a Hindu throughout his life. But then he adopted in his life many points of other religions also, which impressed him very much. In this sometimes he went to such an extent that people so often really confused whether he was a Hindu, a Jain, a Buddhist, a Christian or a Muhammaden. In this regard J. J. Doke wrote about him in 1909, "A very few days ago, I was told that he is a Buddhist. Not long since, a Christian newspaper described him

as a 'Christian Mohammaden', an extraordinary mixture indeed.....
I question whether any system of religion can absolutely hold him.
His views are too closely allied to Christianity to be entirely Hindu,
and too deeply saturated with Hinduism to be called a Christian,
while his sympathies are so wide and collective that one would
imagine he has reached a point where the formulas of sets are
meaningless."[6]

But Gandhi never liked to relinquish his affiliation to Hinduism.
He rather openly said that he loved Hinduism more than anything
else and he was really proud of being a Hindu. When in 1947 an
American correspondent asked Gandhi as to why he preferred
remaining a Hindu when he had so much love and regard for
religions like Christianity and Islam, Gandhi replied, "Believing as
I do in the influence of Heredity, being born in a Hindu family, I
have remained a Hindu. I should reject it if I found it inconsistent
with my moral sense or spiritual growth. On examination I have
found it to be most tolerant of all religions known to me. Its freedom
from dogma makes a forcible appeal to me in as much as it gives
the votary the largest scope for self-expression. Not being an
exclusive religion, it enables followers of that faith not merely to
respect other religions, but it also enables them to admire and
assimilate whatever may be good in other faiths. Non-violence is
common to all the religions, but it has found the highest expression
and application in Hinduism (I do not regard Jainism or Buddhism
as separate from Hinduism). Hinduism believes in the oneness not
merely of all human life but in the oneness of all that lives. Its
worship of cow is, in my opinion, it's unique contribution to the
evolution of humanitarianism. It is a practical application of the
belief in the oneness and therefore in the secrets of all life."[7]

From the above, we can well gather that amidst all his
engagements and pursuits, Gandhi was at bottom a religious man
and he was basically aiming at a religious goal. However, his
outward activities were many sided and he played various roles

of a social worker and reformer, of a politician, of an educationist of an economist and so on. He not only played active role in these spheres but also held definite views on different aspects and spears of human life, which, as we have said earlier, crystalised in some of his key concepts like those of God, man, *ahimsā, satyāgraha, swarāj, swadeshi,* trusteeship etc. These concepts are all related to various aspects of human life. Some are moral and religious concepts, some are social and political and some are economic in nature. All these concepts were formed under various influences of which, quite naturally, the religious influences where the most prominent. Gandhi was, no doubt primarily influenced by Hinduism, but the impact of various other religions on him cannot be ignored. He was fond of reading various religious texts from his very youth and by a sympathetic reading of all of them he became convinced that all religions basically preached the same truth. He learnt about the life and teachings of the Buddha by going through Edwin Arnold's *The Light of Asia*. He read the *Bhagavad Gitā* through its English translation, *To Song Celestial*, by the same author. Both these books left a lasting impression upon his mind. He read the *New Testament* of the *Bible* and was really moved by the teachings of Sermon on the Mount. Everybody knows that the <u>*Gitā*</u> was the life blood of Mahatma Gandhi and he took it as his daily consulting dictionary. But when he went through the Sermon on the Mount, he was so much impressed by it that he said that if per chance he forget everything of the Geeta, he would feel like missing nothing provided someone gave him a copy of the Sermon on the Mount. He saw a basic unity beneath the teachings of the Buddha, the *Geeta* and the Sermon on the Mount. He has himself said in this connection, "My young mind tried to unify the teachings of the *Gitā, The Light of Asia* and *The Sermon on the Mount*."[8] He learnt about Muhammad's life and his ways through Carlyle's *Heroes and Hero-Worship* and through Irving's *Life of Muhammad and his Successors*. These books gave him an idea about the greatness, bravery, austerity, simplicity and humbleness of Muhammad and the sufferings of his successors Hassan and Hussain. He also read the teachings of Muhammad in the Quran. The teaching of all these books and other religious texts had a great impact on Gandhi who was basically a man of religious temperament. All his basic concepts, therefore, bear a definite impression of the different religions of the world. To cite a few instances for illustration the Christian concept of God as love and the following gospel contained in the Sermon on the Mount, 'But I say unto you that ye resist not evil by evil, but who soever smite thee on thy right cheek, turn to him the other also', had a decisive effect on Gandhi in the formation of the positive impact of the concept of *Ahimsā*. Similarly in the Christian cross, Gandhi found a true example of self-suffering for the shake of Truth and this influenced him much in the formation of his concept of *Satyāgraha* as well as of *ahimsā*. Again, the Christian idea of the love of one's neighbour as one self seems to have given a definite hint to Gandhi for his doctrine of *Swadeshi*. The idea of religious tolerance (*sambhāva*) which Gandhi so formally cherished seems to have been impressed upon him by the general Hindu attitude of tolerance towards other religions as well as by the Jain doctrine of *anekāntavad* and *syādvād*. His conception of God although basically formed under Hindu beliefs and ideas was also influenced by the strict monotheism of Islam, the Christian conception of God as love and the ideas present in the Buddhism. He took the atheism of Buddhism as one special kind of theism in which the Moral law itself was taken as God. Under its influence Gandhi sometimes characterised God as the Law and said that the Law maker and his Law are one and the same. His conception of religion which is essentially moral in nature was also much influenced by Buddhism. He was again very much impressed by the concept of brotherhood as present in Islam.

The chief aim of the present work will be to mark and assess the extent to which the various religions of the world influenced

Gandhi in the formation of his various concepts. His concepts of God, man, religion, truth, *ahimsā, satyāgraha, sarvodaya, swarāj, swadeshi*, bread-labour and trusteeship will all be analysed here and attempt will be made to see how far religions of the world have contributed towards the formation of these concepts. We have said above that Gandhi was influenced in his thoughts and ideas not solely and exclusively by the various religions of the world, but also from several other quarters. The impact of some of the renowned authors like Ruskin and Tolstoy was very decisive on Gandhi. But it has to be emphasised that Gandhi, basically religious man, drew the mean impetus and much of the materials for the formation of his concepts from his study and understanding of the various religions of the world. We are of the firm opinion that all his concepts have at bottom some moral or religious tinge and they have been formed under the primary impact of the important principles of the great living religions of the world, of which Hinduism claims the major share, although the importance of the parts played by other religions can neither be ignored not minimised.

But in being influenced by the different religions of the world in the formation of his thoughts and ideas, Gandhi did not always take them in the way or sense they are usually taken and understood by their followers. He rather understood and interpreted them sometimes in his own way and also criticised their followers for not taking the principles of their religion in the right perspective. Specially in case of Hinduism, he took it to be his right and duty to criticise it whenever and wherever he felt that its beliefs were not true to the principles of reason. Although he was a Hindu, a *sanātani* Hindu, as he himself sometimes said, it did not mean that he took all the Hindu beliefs and ideas in exactly the same form in which they were usually accepted at his own time. He worked as a re-interpreter of Hinduism and tried to rid it of many of its superstitions and unreasonable beliefs. So before studying the influence of various religions on Gandhi's thought, we shall first try to present his own understanding and interpretation of the different religions of the world. We shall do this work in our second chapter. In the rest of the chapters we shall try to analyse his important concepts in order to mark out the impact of various religions in their formation. In our final chapter we shall try to present a general assessment of Gandhi's belief and ideas in the context of some of our lurking problems–social, political, economic etc.

We should try to make this study conceptual and analytic and will not be confined to merely noting and recording historical facts and informations about Gandhi and his thought. We shall also try to see the interrelation of concepts so that the question of their mutual consistency may be assessed and examined. Gandhi is so often accused of not being a consistent thinker, because apparently he seems to have made different statements on different occasions on the same point. Gandhi's own statement in this connection also seems to vindicate the above complaint of his readers, "At the time of writing I never think of what I have said before. My aim is not to be consistent with my previous statements on a particular question, but to be consistent with truth as it may present itself to me at a given moment."[9] This statement of Gandhi seems clearly to vindicate the doubt of the complaints that Gandhi never bothered for consistency in his thought. But this is not true. Gandhi's statements may not sometimes prove to be mutually consistent in the strict formal since, but there is a consistency of matter and spirit running throughout his thought. What we mean by saying so is that Gandhi's statements are the results of some of his basic convictions which he so unflinchingly cherished. It is true that these convictions are the results of deep impact of Hinduism and various other religions made upon him, but having once cherished them, he has all along been strictly and unflinchingly guided by them. Therefore there is no question of his beliefs or statements being mutually inconsistent or contradictory. His statement quoted above forms only a part of his full statement. If the full statement is quoted one may see through it what kind of consistency Gandhi aimed at and how the aim of that kind has never been frustrated or belied. The full statement in continuity with the above runs thus, "..... The result has been that I have grown from truth to truth; I have saved my memory and undue strain; and what is more, whenever I have been obliged to compare my writing even to fifty years ago with the latest, I have discovered no inconsistency between the two. But friends who observe inconsistency will do well to take the meaning that my latest writing may yield unless, of course, they prefer the old. But before making the choice they should try to see if there is not an underlying and abiding consistency between the two seeming inconsistencies."[10]

Gandhi believed in his principles absolutely but he also believed that man being shrouded by limitations could know it only in a relative manner. He took truth as absolute but men according to him, could know it only relatively. Hence man's idea of truth had always a scope to grow. It could never be fixed and static. Similarly, a moral principle like that of *ahimsā* was to be cherished absolutely, but actual practical occasions might demand concessions and men being men, must have to concede to the demands of the occasion. So, in a sense, Gandhi was a moral relativist, although he believed in his moral principles absolutely. His convictions were absolute and he hardly ever liked to compromise with them easily.

From the above it seems clear that Gandhi was basically a religious man. But this should not give us an occasion to ignore the multidimensional personality of Gandhi and the multiple nature of roles that he played in his life. This may be clear to a great extent by the following statements of Raghavan Iyer which we would like to quote here, "He was the heroic champion of human rights in South Africa; the revolutionary leader of a mass movement for political freedom; a crusader against untouchability; an experimenter in nature cure, dialectics and education; a reformer much concerned with alcoholism; the exploitation of women and cruelty to animals; a student of comparative religion and practical unity amongst them; as killed lawyer and draftsman of petition and memoranda; a prolific correspondent who gave moral guidance to thousands of people in many countries; the founder of several *āshrams* and communal settlements; the author of a few book and pamphlets and thousands upon thousands of articles on a great variety of subjects; something of a mystic and a monk-definitely an ascetic figure pledged to several exacting vows, including the vow of non-possession; a daring, though not a systematic, political thinker."[11]

However, despite and beyond all, Gandhi was definitely a religious man, but not only in the sense of being a *sanātani* Hindu or in the sense of being a true observer of the essential points of all the living religions of the world, but in a far deeper sense. He was religious in the sense of being a true reconciliator between theory and practice, between concepts and its practical application between conviction and life truly up to it, between faith and unflinching adherence to it. What we mean to say here is that religion, to our mind, is the way of life adopted in thought, speech and action with a sense of total determination, honesty and sincerity, i.e., in brief, with a sense of total commitment. And Gandhi's life is an ideal example of it.

References

1. *Speeches and writings of Mahatma Gandhi*, Appendix II, p. 40
2. *Young India*, Vol. III, p. 350
3. M.K.Gandhi, *An Autobiography*, (Beacon Press, Boston, 1966) p. XII
4. *Harijan*, August, 1936

5. *The Collected Works of Mahatma Gandhi,* (Navajivan, 1958, Vol. 10) pp. 20-21

6. J. J. Doke, *M. K. Gandhi* (Natesan, 1909) p. 142

7. *Harijan,* January 1936

8. *An Autobiography, p. 16*

9. *Harijan,* September, 1936

10. *Ibid*

11. Raghavan N. Iyer, *The Moral and Political Thought of Mahatma Gandhi,* (Oxford univ. Press, 1938, Paperback) p. 5

Content

Chapter-I

Gandhi's understanding of Different Religions

Gandhi was essentially a religious man and his religion was Hinduism. But he tried to assimilate in his ideas the good points of almost all the important religions of the world. In his view there was no conflict amongst the different religions of the world. There was rather ample scope for mutual understanding amongst them. All of them at bottom referred to the same truth. Therefore Gandhi did not see any contradiction in being a Hindu, rather a *sanātani* Hindu, as he said, and at the same time observing the good and essential points of various other religions such as Buddhism, Jainism, Christianity, Islam etc. But Gandhi did not always take the various beliefs and practices associated with different religions in the same form in which their followers normally took them. He had his own understanding and interpretation of the various points related with different religions and in this he mostly based his ideas on the original text or the original statements of the founders of the religions concerned. For example, in understanding Christianity he did not so much base his ideas on what was mostly or generally invoked in the name of Christianity as on what Jesus Christ is reported to have said and on what is written in the Bible. Similarly, in interpreting Islam he was guided not by what the Muslims were actually doing in the name of Islamic faith and religion but by the message and summons contained in the different surahs of the Quran and the various utterances which Mohammad himself is reported to have made at times. He was also guided by the historical reports of the ways of life that were followed by such prophets as Muhammad or

Jesus Christ. In interpreting Hinduism, he was rather ruthless, critical and in a sense very radical. Gandhi, it is true, often expressed his devotion and respect for Hinduism and also felt proud of being a Hindu. He seemed to have a very respectful attitude towards the Hindu religious text such as the Vedas the Upanishads, the Purānas, the Rāmāyana, the Mahābhārata and most of all, the Bhagavad Gitā. But it is also true that he did not hesitate to criticise such aspects of Hinduism which did not appeal to his reason. He was, for example, very much critical of the treatment meted out to the *shudrās* based on the sanctions of some of the *Dharmasutrās* and *Dharmashāstrās,* although at the same time he expressed his firm faith in the *Varna Dharm,* which formed part of Hinduism right from the age of the Vedas. Gandhi felt himself to be more justified and free in criticising Hinduism rather than other religions, because, according to him, one had the right to criticise the non-appealing or irrational aspects of one's own religion. But it was unfair, according to him, to criticise the faiths of others. This attitude of Gandhi was fully in keeping with the spirit of the science of comparative religion. It was also in consonance with his attitude of religious tolerance and secularism. Now before we see the impact of the different religions on the various aspects of Gandhi's thought we shall make a brief survey of Gandhi's understanding of the important aspects of various religions which influenced him in some significant way. Let us take the different religions one by one :

(A) HINDUISM

In a sense Hinduism is a peculiar religion as compared to other religions of the world. Unlike other religions it has neither any definite origin nor any definite founder prophet. It also does not have any one specific sacred textbook to which one may always refer as the complete basis of Hinduism. It has no definite creeds and no specific rituals. Varying beliefs and practices may be found amongst those who call themselves Hindus. A Hindu may be a polytheist, or a monotheist or a monist or even an atheist. Hinduism is really a vast and apparently incoherent religious complex. It is rightly characterised as a vast jungle in which it is very difficult to mark out how many kinds of trees and plants flourish. In fact, to summarise the main principles, beliefs and practices of any religion is very difficult, but in the case of Hinduism, it seems impossible. The universalistic outlook of Hinduism forms the very basis of its philosophy of religion. According to it there is only one basic reality underlying everything which is differently named in different religions. All the different religions are like different paths leading to the same goal. So there is no question of preserving any rigid set of principles or practices. Everyone has got the right to follow his own path and approach God in his own way. Hinduism never claims that a particular prophet is *the* prophet and a particular faith is *the* faith. It does not believe in inflicting rigid rules of prayer, worship etc. As a matter of fact Hinduism speaks of various ways of approaching God or of attaining salvation. There are, broadly speaking, three such ways—the way of knowledge *(jnāna mārg)*, the way of action *(karma mārg)* and the way of devotion *(bhakti mārg)*. Anyone according to his temperament may adopt any of these paths and attain his final spiritual end. Hinduism is in its spirit against any rigid rules of religion. It is very liberal in its approach and outlook. Gandhi himself was very much aware of this liberal and universalistic outlook of Hinduism. This is evident from his various remarks, some of which are as below: "Hinduism is not an exclusive religion. In it there is room for the worship of all prophets of the world. It is not a missionary religion in the ordinary sense of term..... Hinduism tells everyone to worship God according to his faith or *dharma*, and so lives at peace with all religion."[1] Again, "Hinduism is not a codified religion. We have in Hinduism hundreds and thousands of books whose names even we do not know, which go under the name *shāstra*."[2] As Hinduism is not bound under rigid dogmatic rules and has been always accommodative in its character and spirit, so much so that various religions and cultures have merged into it from time to time. Its nature is not fixed, rather it has an evolutionary character. Gandhi has pointed to this aspect of Hinduism when he says, "Hinduism is a grand evolutionary process and not a narrow creed..... Hinduism is a living organism liable to growth and decay, and subject to this law of nature. One and indivisible at the root it has grown into a vast tree with innumerable branches. The changes in the season affected. It has its autumn and summer winter and spring."[3]

Now, although Hinduism is a very broad and liberal religion admitting of no specific creeds, rigid rules, etc., it should not be regarded as having no distinguishing character of its own. Certain basic features of it can still be marked out in almost all of which Gandhi firmly believed as a Hindu. Although Hinduism is not essentially theistic in the technical sense, by and large it accepts God and his different incarnations. Some of the other characteristic beliefs associated with Hinduism are: Belief in the authority of the *Vedas* and the *Upanishads* as well as in some other sacred text such as the *Rāmāyana*, the *Mahābhārata*, the *Bhagwat Gitā*, etc., belief in the immortality of soul, belief in the law of *karma* and rebirth, belief in the possibility of *Moksha* etc. Some of the Hindu practices consists in observing such ethical virtues as *satya, ahimsā, brahmacharya, asteya, aparigraha* etc. Gandhi firmly entertained all these beliefs and also sincerely acted according to them According to him, to be a Hindu is to believe in God, the immortality of the soul, transmigration, the law of *karma, moksha* etc. and to try to practice truth and *ahimsā* in daily life. In its social aspect Hinduism is much known for its *Varnāshrama dharma*. According to it Hindu society consists of four different classes—*Brahmana, Kshatriya, Vaishya* and *Shudra:* and every individual living in the Hindu society has to pass through for successive stages of life—*Brahmacharya, Gārhasthya, Vānaprastha and Sannyāsa*. The former is specifically called *Varna dharma* and the latter *Āshram dharma*. Gandhi firmly believed in this Hindus scheme of social order and individual mode of living. Besides he also cherished some of the popular Hindu beliefs such as the sacredness and the protection of the cow, the idol worship etc. Gandhi called himself a *sanātani* Hindu and by way of explaining why he called himself so, he said, "I call myself *sanātani* Hindu because, (1) I believe in the Vedas, Upanishads, the Purānas and all that goes by the name of Hindu scriptures and therefore in avatars and rebirth; (2) I believe in the *Varnāshrama dharm* in a sense, in my opinion, strictly Vedic but not in its present popular and crude sense; (3) I believe in the protection of the cow in its much larger sense than the popular; (4)

I do not disbelieve in idol worship."[4] The point amply shows how Gandhi believed in the essentials as well as certain popular ideas and practices of Hinduism. However, some of the points noted above need clarification. Gandhi believed in the *Varnāshrama dharma* in its Vedic sense. Here Gandhi seems to have made a specific reference to the Varna dharma. The first mention of the *Varna dharma* is in the *Purusha Sukta* of the *Rigveda,* where the four *Varnas* have been described as having sprung from the four different parts of the body of the Creative Spirit. The *Brāhmins* are said to have sprung from the head of the spirit, the *Kshatriya* out of his arms, the *Vaishyas* out of his thighs and the *Shūdras* out of the feet.[5] This poetic image, as Dr. Radhakrishnan says, "is intended to convey the organic character of the society."[6] To say the same thing in a few more words, the imagery intends to convey that the different *varnas* are the different inevitable limbs of the same social organism. Just as the different parts of an organism are all important in their own ways and the organism cannot function properly without any of them, similarly, the different *varnas* are all important in their own ways for the social organism and each of them has its proper role to play for the upkeep and development of the society and none can be regarded as superior or inferior. Curse to the posterity which interpreted the *varna dharma* rather perversely and let it degenerate into the cast system with several vices. When Gandhi was referring to the Vedic sense of the word *dharma,* he was really referring to that organic aspect of each one in which each one was of equal value and each one had its respectable place in the society. Later on, its degeneration into the cast system gave birth to the vice of untouchability which, according to Gandhi, was a slur on Hinduism and which he could never tolerate. It is well known that Gandhi throughout his life fought for the so-called untouchables, the *shudras* and renamed them as '*Harijans*' the people of God. He was never ready to believe that Hinduism in its true spirit did ever make any room for a class of people being treated as untouchables.

By advocating the cause of the protection of cow in a larger sense Gandhi really advocated the cause of the protection of all living creatures. Cow was just a symbol of the sub-human species, according to him. In his strict conformity with his belief in *ahimsā* Gandhi cherished a strong sense of love and compassion not only for human beings but also for animals and other sub-human species. Cow protection, according to him, symbolises the protection of all living beings, especially those who were weak, meek and helpless. The Hindu belief in the sacredness of the cow and the strong sense of the Hindus to protect the cow at all cost were taken by Gandhi as a symbol of the Hindu sense of not killing not only the human beings but also the animals. Animals deserved our compassion, love and sympathy as much as the human beings. On acount of this sentiment, many Hindus since the ancient days have not been meat eaters. This cow protection according to Gandhi is really a symbol of the Hindu belief in the basic oneness of all creatures—human and subhuman. Gandhi's exact sense of cow protection can be seen in his following statement, "The cow protection which can bring in *moksha* must from its very nature, include the protection of everything that feels. Therefore, in my opinion, every little breach of the *ahimsā* principle like causing hurt by harsh speech to anyone man women or child, to cause pain to the weakest and the most insignificant creature on earth, would be tantamount to the sin of beef-eating, differing from it in degree, if at all, rather than in kind. That being so, I hold that with all our passion let loose we cannot today claim to be following the principle of cow protection."[7]

Idol worship is very much in practice amongst the Hindus and many people decry it as a mark of primitivism. But Gandhi never decried it and pointed out that in one very important sense it was religiously viable. To quote Gandhi in this regard, "An idol does not excite any feeling of veneration in me. But I think that idol worship is a part of human nature. We hanker after symbolism..... Images are an aid to worship. No Hindu considers an image to be God. I do not consider idol worship as sin." The idol works as a symbol of deity through which the devotee wants to establish a lively relationship with the latter. It is very difficult for the ordinary man to pay his oblation to and establish a relationship with the deity in abstraction. In the idol, he finds a medium through which such a relationship becomes possible. Every Hindu knows that the stone idol is not God, it is simply a symbol, a medium. As Gandhi himself said, "Every Hindu child knows that the stone in the famous temple of Banaras is not Kashi Vishwanath. But he believes that the Lord of the universe does reside especially in the stone."[8] According to Gandhi, we should, of course, not make a fetish of the idol; that must be treated as merely, a symbol a medium. So long as we remember this fact there is nothing wrong about idol worship. This kind of idol-worship is not ideal idolatry, it becomes so only when we make a fetish of the idol. Here Gandhi's approach seems very near to that of Paul Tillich,[9] a famous modern American theologian. Of course, Tillich's approach is theological and that of Gandhi's practical, but still there is a similarity between the two in as much as both of them recognise the role of symbols in religion as valuable media for our establishing a relation with the deity. Like Tillich, Gandhi also recognised that symbols point beyond themselves and at the same time they partake of the nature of the reality which they point to. And so Gandhi never denounced the worship of idols by most of the Hindus.

Gandhi was much impressed by the Hindu belief in the unity of all existence and the essentially ethical and spiritual outlook of Hinduism. Everything, according to it, is the manifestation of the same divine spirit. The *Brahman* or *Ātman* is present in everything. So there is a basic unity amongst all existence of the world. It is in this sense that Gandhi believed in *Advaita*, i. e, in absolute oneness of all being. He said, "The chief value of Hinduism lies in holding the actual belief that all life (not only human beings but all sentient beings) is one, i.e., all life coming from one universal source, call it Allah, God or *Parmeshwar*.... This unity of life is a peculiarity of Hinduism which confines salvation not to human beings alone but says that it is possible for all of God's creatures."[10] On account of this belief in the unity of all existence, Gandhi preached love even towards inanimate nature and was very much against the technological exploitation of nature which is characteristic of the modern western civilization. Thus Gandhi interpreted the *Advaita* of Hinduism in his own way and understood it as a principle of the absolute unity or oneness of entire existence. The same spirit or the same *Brahman* runs, according to him, through each and every atom of the world. He was very much impressed by the famous

Gitā saying, "When one sees Me everywhere and everything in Me, I am never lost to him and he is never lost to Me."[11]

As we have said above, Gandhi was also very much impressed by the essentially ethical and spiritual outlook of Hinduism. He appreciated the Vedic conception of *Rta* according to which the world has a moral basis and it was strictly governed by a moral law. The Hindu belief in the law of *karma* is a consequence of this Vedic concept of the *Rta* itself. The concept of *Dharma* as present in the ancient Hindu *shāstrās* also had much impact upon him. Of course, he neither liked nor wanted to go in the cumbrous details of the *dharmas* as given in the *Dharmashastras,* but then he accepted their general moral import. He took *dharmas* as the basic foundation of the universe. Without it the universe could not exist. Gandhi found the Hindu sacred books right from the Vedas as filled with precious moral virtues and duties. *Ahimsā* was one of the virtues which found its first explicit expression in the *Chhāndogya Upanishad.* Later on it has found expression in the various *Dharmasutras* and *Dharmashāstra.* Patanjali's *Yogasutra* explicitly mentions it as one of the five *yamas.* Similarly, the virtue of *satya*, on which Gandhi lead utmost emphasis, has been taken as the greatest virtue right from the age of the *Rig Veda.* Sometimes, there is explicit mention in the Vedas that *satya* constitutes the content of the *Rta.* The other ethical virtues such as love, passion, self-sacrifice celibacy, selflessness, liberty etc. have been repeatedly emphasised in the various Hindu texts and all these have definite impact on Gandhi's thought.

The Hindu outlook towards world and life has been characteristically spiritual. Apart from the Chārvākas, even those systems of Hindu thought which do not believe in God, have a definite belief in the existence of an immortal soul in man and they take spiritual attainment in the form of *Moksha* as the highest attainment. Hinduism has always made a distinction between the material and the spiritual and has believed in the supremacy and ultimacy of the latter. In the words of Dr. Radhakrishnan, "Real religion can exist without definite conception of deity but not without a distinction between the spiritual and the profane, the sacred and the secular.... There are systems of Hindu thought like the *Sāmkhya* and the Jain which do not admit God but affirm the reality of the spiritual consciousness. There are theists like Ramanuja for whom the spiritual consciousness, though not God himself, is the only way in which God can be known. All, however, are agreed in regarding salvation as the attainment of the true status of the individual."[12] Thus Hinduism on the whole accords supreme value to the spiritual and not to the material. This aspect of Hinduism was very much liked by Gandhi and he took it as his guiding principle. His entire thought is besmeared with this Hindu spiritual ideal.

It was due to such elements present in Hinduism that Gandhi loved it so passionately and felt proud of being a Hindu. He loved and praised many other religions, rather all the religions of the world because he felt that all of them were directed towards the same truth. But he had a special love and regard for Hinduism. The great intensity of Gandhi's love for Hinduism can very well be measured through his following statement: "I can no more describe my feeling for Hinduism then for my wife. She moves me as no other women in the world can. Not that she has no faults. I dare say that she has many more than I see myself. But the feeling of an indissoluble bond is there. Even so I feel about Hinduism with all its fouls and limitations. Nothing elates me so much as the music of the *Gitā* or the *Rāmāyana* of *Tulsidās.*"[14] Hinduism might have certain limitations, as any other religion of the world might have, but still Gandhi felt an indissoluble bond with the Hindu religion-partly because of his heredity and partly because of the many points that Hinduism uniquely held to its credit. Gandhi was also conscious of the various assaults done on Hinduism at times by foreign invaders, but he felt that there was something unique in it which kept it alive in spite of these onslaughts. Hinduism is known as *sanātana dharma*, and according to Gandhi, there was something really *sanātana* (permanent or eternal) in it which has been able to maintain it and keep it alive. The main factor that has kept Hinduism alive even today, according to him, is its unshakable faith in spiritualism as well as its universal and philanthropic character.

From whatever we have said above about Gandhi's understanding of and love for Hinduism, one may have the impression, and perhaps a correct one, that Gandhi was a traditionalist and he believed in traditional Hinduism in the form it was depicted in various ancient *shāstra* or in the form in which it has been traditionally accepted and followed. But this is not literally true. Gandhi was in many respects very much radical in his approach and he did not hesitate in criticising those aspects of Hinduism which did not appeal to his reason. Many times he felt that Hinduism, as commonly viewed, was not the pure and real Hinduism: it was, as he said, a 'parody' of that. Gandhi, as a matter of facts, was more an interpreter and reformer of Hinduism than a traditional believer of it. Of course he was very much impressed by the essential ethical and spiritual outlook of traditional Hinduism, but then he was also a staunch critic of many of the unhealthy practices prevalent in Hinduism. For example, he was very much against the caste system prevalent in Hinduism. Untouchability was a direct consequence of this system and this he hated most intensely. As we have seen above, he was not against the *varnadharma* as depicted in the Vedas, but he could not accept that the vice of untouchability had any place in this *varna dharma*. This vice was not in any way consistent with the essential spirit of Hinduism, which took all living beings, rather the entire existence, as basically one on account of there being the manifestation of the same divine spirit. Gandhi regarded untouchability as a slur on Hinduism and sometimes went to the extent of saying that if untouchability was to remain a part and parcel of Hinduism, he would better cease to be a Hindu. But then he firmly believed that Hinduism, understood in its essential and real spirit, could have no genuine place for such a vice. To those few who wanted to justify this vice by quoting a few Sanskrit verses from here and there, Gandhi said, "He is no *sanātani* Hindu who is narrow, bigoted and considers evil to be good if it has the sanction of authority and is to be found in any Sanskrit book."[15] Gandhi was sometimes very radical and yet perfectly rational. He did not accept each and every word of the Shastras literally. He tested this saying on his touchstone of truth and accepted only those which successfully stood this test. As he said, "Whatever falls from Truth should be rejected, no matter where it comes from: therefore the burden lies on the shoulders of that person who upholds a practice which is inconsistent with the Truth: so that if a man wants to defend, for instance, untouchability, he has to show that it is consistent with Truth. Unless he shows that all the authorities that we miss cite in support of it are irrelevant."[16] Clearly Gandhi was referring here to such people who sometimes quoted from the various *Dharmsutras* and *Dharmshāstras* such as the *Dharmasutras* of Gautam and the *Mānava Dharmashāstra*, where a very low status has been given to the *shudrās*. Gandhi was not going to yield to the authority of such *sutras* for upholding untouchability as a genuine feature of Hindu religion or culture. He was guided by the essential spirit of Hinduism, and not by a few verses present in some *shastras*. He clearly said that he was not a 'literalist'. He tried to understand the spirit of the various scriptures of the world and not the literal meaning of each and every word and sentence present there in. In connection with the story of the *shudra* allegedly punished by Ramchandra for learning the Veda (Veda learning is prohibited for the *shudras* by the shastras), Gandhi expressed his reaction in the following words, ".... I do not swear by every word that is to be found in so many editions published as the book of *Rāmāyana* of Tulsidas. It is the spirit running through the book that holds me spell-bound. I cannot myself subscribe to the prohibition against shudras learning the Vedas.... knowledge cannot be the prerogative of any class or section...."[17] Gandhi always cautioned people against being a blind follower of each and every word of a sacred text. He advised to apply reason and not to take what was not in accordance with the reason as true. Gandhi, thus, was a rationalist and not a dogmatic traditionalist. He very clearly asserted, "I cannot let a spiritual text supersede my reason. Whilst I believe that the principal books are inspired, they suffer from a process of double distillation. Firstly, they come through a human profile, and then through the commentaries of interpreters. Nothing in them comes from God directly..... I cannot surrender my reason while I subscribe to divine revelation. And above all, 'the letter killeth, the spirit giveth life."[18]

Along with the *shudras*, the women have also been treated very badly in many of the Hindu *shāstras*. They have also been given very low status in Hindu society. Gandhi was very much against the social evil also. He always fought for the equality of status for women. Women are as much human beings as men were and there was no reason why the former should be given a lower status in the society. Gandhi took this discrimination as one of the greatest evils of Hindu social life. He said, "Of all the evils for which man has made himself responsible, none is so degrading shocking or so brutal as his abuse of the better half of humanity—to me the female sex, not the weaker sex."[19] Gandhi had every praise for the meekness, humbleness and lovingness of the women and he took them to with the real incarnation of *ahimsā*. He said, "If non-violence is the law of our being, the future is with women.... God has vouchsafed to women the power of non-violence more than to man..... Women are the natural messenger of the gospel of non-violence if only they will realise their high state."[20]

Gandhi not only brought about many social reforms in Hinduism, but he also tried to analyse some of the basic concepts of Hindu religion in his own way. For example, although he accepted the Hindu belief in the existence of God and the various *Avatāras,* he analyses the Hindu concept of God in his own way. He made the two concepts god & truth identical. We shall discuss the identity of God and truth in great detail in the coming chapters and therefore we shall not say anything more about this point here. At any rate what we have said above is enough to indicate that although Gandhi was a staunch Hindu, he did not always understood Hinduism and its various concepts in the way in which they were traditionally understood.

(B) JAINISM

Hinduism, Buddhism and Jainism are allied religions and their essentials, by and large, are very much the same. Gandhi was fully alive to the basic unity of the three religions and he sometimes explicitly expressed that he did not consider Buddhism and Jainism as completely independent of or separate from Hinduism. It is not surprising therefore that Jainism also had its full impact on Gandhi. And it is very clear that quite a number of his beliefs and practices bear the impression of Jain philosophy and religion. Raghav, N. Iyer in his book *The Moral and Political Thought of Mahatma Gandhi* reports of a reminiscence of Ajgaonkar in which the latter relates one of his conversions with Tilak in the following words, "Tilak asked me: 'What is Gandhi's cast?' I replied, 'Gandhi is a *vaisya* by cast and a *Vaishnava* by religion.' Tilak looked surprised and replied: 'It is strange that up to now I did not know Gandhi's religion. People will laugh at my ignorance about such a great man. I was under the impression that Gandhi was a Jain because all his opinions and teachings favour the Jain religion. Non-violence, *satyāgraha*, fasting etc. all these are more in keeping with Jain teachings than the Hindu religion."[21] The extract amply shows what kind of impression Jainism must have cast on Gandhi such that a personality like Tilak also took him to be a Jain by religion. And this is quite natural. Of all the states of India, Gujarat was most influenced at that time (and perhaps even now is most influenced) by Jain religion; and Gandhi's father, though a *vaishnava* by faith had very frequently contacted with Jain monks. Stephen Hay points out that Gandhi was influenced by the ideas and the living examples of the members of the Jain faith whom Gandhi came to know as a boy and a young man."[22]

It is well known that Jainism along with Buddhism originated in India as a reaction against caste discrimination and excessive ritualism prevalent in Hinduism. We have seen that Gandhi was very much against caste distinctions and therefore it is quite natural that he should have very great love and respect for Jainism. Gandhi himself did not like a religion of excessive ritualism, He preferred a religion which was moralistic and spiritualistic in character and Jainism fulfilled both these conditions. This religion is concerned with moral conduct and rituals, ceremonies etc. do not have any place in it. However, what influenced Gandhi most was the Jain belief that everything, big or small has a soul, strengthened Gandhi's doctrine of non-violence and love. Stephen Hay very much stressed the point that Gandhi's idea of non-violence was basically influenced by the Jain concept of *Jiva*.[23] Because everything had a soul, through which greater or less degree of consciousness, it was unjust and sinful to harm or injure any creature. Non-violence must be a universal law. But then Gandhi was sometimes critical of the excessive emphasis given by the Jains upon non-violence and the very rigid observance of the vow by the Jain monks. Gandhi believed that the extreme emphasis laid by the Jains was based on the false impression that the agony of death was more severe than the agonies of the lifetime. Moreover Gandhi believed that the undue emphasis upon the sacredness of the sub-human life in preference to human life led to a distortion of the real meaning and spirit of *ahimsā*. Thus although Gandhi was very much influenced by the Jain doctrine of *ahimsā*, he did not like the way in which the doctrine was practiced in Jainism. The Jaina doctrine of soul mentioned above no doubt paved the way for universal love, and Gandhi did appreciate it, but he did not like to make a fetish of *ahimsā*.

Let us see some of the main principles of Jainism which has definite impact on Gandhi. Gandhi was influenced not only by the religion but also by some of the important philosophical principles of Jainism namely, *Anekāntavad, Syādvad,* and *sāpekshavād* (relativism). The doctrine of *anekāntvad* envisages that every object has got unfinite number of attributes *(Anantdharmakarmvastuh)* and it is rather impossible for any ordinary human being to know all of them. Only some of them is known to a person at a particular time. And hence nobody can claim to have complete knowledge. What we are able to know, therefore, is only the relative truth and not the absolute truth. All our judgments *(nyaya)* about objects must be preceded by the prefix '*Syād*' (relatively speaking), which signifies that whatever we speak or write about can claim only relative truth. We must never insist that what we know about anything is the only truth, the absolute truth and what others say about it is simply wrong or mistaken. What is true is that all of us may be true from our own respective standpoints. Truth is not the privilege of any single human being and it is acquired only relatively. Our status in the world is comparable, according to Jainism, to that of the six blind people who separately touched only one part of an elephant and characterised the animal in terms of that part exclusively. As they were depicting only a part of the truth from their own respective standpoints so we also know only the partial truth and not the whole truth about anything. We must grant value and weight to other's opinion and must never try to belittle the knowledge of others. We should be tolerant and accommodative in matters of knowledge and judgement. Gandhi wholeheartedly shared the above viewpoint of Jainism and acted according to it throughout his life. As a matter of fact the above viewpoint regarding knowledge, judgment and truth contains within it the germs or spirit of true non-violence. We can very well say that the Jain relativism as manifested in its doctrine of *anekāntvād* and *syādvād* is the logical counterpart of the ethical virtue of non-violence. To give no value to other's opinion and to declare them to be wrong are, in a way, to offend him and this goes against the true spirit of non-violence. Non-violence in Jainism does not simply mean inflicting physical injury to someone, rather it has a very wide connotation. Offending or hurting anybody in any way, physically or through mere words, is a kind of *himsā* (violence) and that must be avoided. The Jain doctrine of relativism is logically related to this wide connotation of the term non-violence.

Besides non-violence, Jainism lays emphasis on the following ethical virtues-purity, chastity, celibacy, non-attachment, non-possession, non-stealing, truth, compassion, love, fellow feeling etc. But of these utmost emphasis has been laid on the virtues of celibacy (*brahmacharya*), non-attachment (*aparigrah*), non-stealing (*asteya*) and truth (*satya*). These along with non-violence constitute the *panchmahāvrat* of Jainism which has got a very special significance in it. Gandhi has mentioned exactly these five in his list of ethical virtue. Although it cannot be said that in making these five as the primary ethical virtues, Gandhi was borrowing from Jainism (because those virtues are stressed in Hinduism and Buddhism also), still it can safely be said that in giving the detailed analysis of these virtues, Gandhi was indebted more to Jainism than to any other religion. For example, the Jain concept of *ahimsā* is very comprehensive and inclusive and this seems to have a direct effect on Gandhi's understanding of the concept. We shall give below a brief analysis of all the five ethical woes or virtues in the light of the Jain view of them :-

1) **Ahimsā (Non-violence)**-It is the greatest rule of conduct in Jainism. It is understood and practiced in Jainism in a very wide sense. Violence or injury or harm caused to any living being in any form is *himsā*. So *ahimsā* is to be practiced not only in deed, but also in thoughts and words. Keeping ill will against anybody in thought or speaking harsh words to anybody

is as good an example of *himsā* as inflicting any bodily injury to anybody. So mere avoidance of killing somebody is not *ahimsā*. It is very much more besides. Even forcing someone to do something against his will or curtailing somebody's freedom is deemed as *himsā* in Jainism. Causing injury to someone due to negligence is also *himsā*. Negligence *(pramāda)* implies the passion of attachment *(rāga)* and aversion *(dvesha)* and any action done under their is spell is violence. Non-violence understood in such wide sense is the rule of conduct according to Jainism. Practicing *ahimsā* in the Jain sense is not something very easy. It is a kind of *tapas*. On its positive side *ahimas* implies a life of love for all.

2) **Satya (Truthfulness)**-Generally speaking, this rule of conduct enjoins abstinence from giving false statements or avoiding telling a lie. But the mere statement of fact is not truth. Truth, if it is harmful to others should be avoided. It must be spoken with beneficent intentions. Otherwise it will offend or harm somebody and that will be *himsā*. Exaggression of fact, finding fault with others, using indecent speech etc. are all examples of untruth according to Jainism and therefore they must be avoided. Speaking in a noble, beneficent and balanced manner and with a peaceful mind upholds truth and hence it must be practiced accordingly. According to Amrita Chandra, the following are the examples of falsehood and they must be avoided: 1. Denial of the existence of a thing with reference to its position, time and nature, 2. Asserting the existence of a non-existent thing with reference to its position, time and nature, 3. Representing a thing as something else 4. Reprehensible speech, 5. Sinful speech and 6. Unpalatable *(apriya)* speech.

3) **Asteya (Non-stealing)**-Generally speaking, this means abstention from taking someone else, something which is not given. But as a Jain rule of conduct, *asteya* is more comprehensive and includes within it the avoidance of all sorts of dishonesty and conceit. Buying a valuable article at low price, appropriating something that has been forgotten about by its possessor, having greed for the property of others, taking

a thing in one's possession whose ownership is doubtful etc. are all examples of stealing and they must be avoided. Jainism regards stealing as a kind of violence *(himsā)*, because wealth is the external vital force of a person and taking it away without his consent offends or harms him. Even abetment of theft or purchasing of stolen property or doing any kind of illegal business is a kind of stealing according to Jainism, because each such behaviour disposes a rightful owner in some way or other.

4) **Brahmacharya (Celibacy)**-This vow has been much emphasised in Hinduism and Buddhism also, but Jainism lays far more emphasis on it. It extols the life of a celibate or a monk much more than any other religion. This vow or rule of conduct stands for abstinence from sexual intercourse particularly from all sorts of illegal sexual intercourse. *Sāmantabhadra* has included within this vow renunciation of contact with any woman other than one's wife. Not only the actual commitment of adultery is a violation of this vow but also the thought thereof. In general, *brahmacharya* means abstinence from excessive desire for any sort of sins enjoyment. Thinking about such enjoyment is also a violation of the vow.

5) *Aparigrah* **(Non-possession or non-attachment)**-It stands for not only abstinence from excessive material possession but also for the avoidance of desire for such possession. So its exact meaning is non attachment rather than non-possession. Excessive desire for material possession is *parigrah* and it must be avoided. Accumulating more than what one needs for his maintenance is *parigrah* or even *steya*, because in a way it is depriving others of their legitimate rights. Attachment is generated by *moha* and it results in *himsā. Moha* or attraction towards worldly possession must be avoided. For, otherwise, one cannot pursue right conduct. Desire for worldly objects is the root of all evils and therefore it must be shunned.

Jainism advocates a threefold path known as *Triratna* (Three jewels) for the attainment of salvation. Three jewels are Right Faith *(samyagdarshan)*, Right knowledge *(samyaggyān)* and Right conduct *(samyagcharitra)*. The above *panch-mahāvrat* as come under the last jewel, i.e., the right conduct. They are to be followed by every Jain, whether a laity or a monk. Jainism however extols the life of a monk and there are many vows of spiritual and moral purity which are prescribed only for a monk. Fasting has been given an important place amongst Jain *Vratas*. Generally, Jains are required to fast on *ashtami, chaturdashi* and *purnimā* days. Fasting includes not only abstinence from food but also from perfumes, physical adornment, ornaments and sexual intercourse. We shall see in due course what an immense impact these moral and spiritual vows of Jainism had on Mahatma Gandhi's thought.

(C) Buddhism

Like Jainism, Buddhism also originated as a reaction against excessive ritualism and caste distinction of Hinduism. But Buddhism is not very far removed from Hinduism in its essentials. Many, including Gandhi, regard his as an offshoot of Hinduism. Influences of *Upanishads* upon it are quite evident. According to Gandhi the main contribution of Buddhism to Hinduism is the former's negative attitude on sacrifice and it's non-recognition of the caste distinction. As Gandhi has said, "The one thing that Buddha showed India was that God was not a God who can be appeased by the sacrifices of the innocent animals. On the contrary, he held that those who sacrificed animals in the hope of pleasing God were guilty of a double Sin."[24] The second thing that Gautam taught was that all that caste means today as it meant in his time also was wholly wrong. That is to say, he abolished every distinction of superiority and inferiority that was even in his time eating into the vitals of Hinduism.[25] The Buddha formally denounced the custom of regarding someone as superior in cast simply on the ground of his birth. One was really a brāhmin only if he inculcated the virtues of a brāhmin. As the *Dhammapada* says, "Not by matte hair, nor by lineage, not by caste is one brāhmin. He is a brāhmin in whom there exist truth and righteousness. *(Na Jatahina gotten najachchahotibrāhmano. Yamhisachehamcha dhammo cha so cha brāhmano).* [26]Also, "I do not call a man brāhmin because of his origin or of his mother though he is or offered salutation as a brāhmin and is wealthy, but I call him a brāhmin who is poor and free from all attachments *(Na chāham brāhmanambrumiYonijammattisa-mbhavam. Bhovādi nāma so hotisāchehotisakinchano. Akinchanamanādānamtam-ahambrumibrāhmanam).*"[27] So a caste determined by birth was insignificant. What really mattered was one's virtue or quality. No ethically important distinction between man and man would be made on account of birth or lineage.

Buddhism is regarded as atheistic in nature. It is said that the Buddha did not believe in any God and praised a purely ethical religion. His religion is man centered and humanistic instead of being God centred. Apparently this view seems to be quite sound and correct, but Gandhi did not take Buddhism in the above way. To be sure, he did not doubt that Buddhism was a very elevated kind of humanistic religion, but he did not subscribe to the view that Buddha was atheistic. According to Gandhi it is not true that Buddha did not believe in God. What is true is that he did not believe in God as a person who needed sacrifice. According to him, the law itself, i.e., *Dharma* itself was God. God was not separate from his own law. The law and the Lawmaker are one—this, according to Gandhi, was the underlying faith of the Buddha. Therefore he cannot be called an atheist. He believed in God: only, he believed in God as an impersonal law, the law of moral government of the universe. To quote Gandhi's own words, "I have heard it contended times without number and I have read it in books also claiming to express the spirit of Buddhism that Buddha did not believe in God. In my humble opinion, such a belief contradicts the very central fact of Buddha's teaching. In my humble opinion, such a confusion has arisen over his rejection and just reaction of all the base things that passed in his generation in the name of God.... His whole soul rose in mighty indignation against the belief that are being called God, required for his satisfaction the living blood of animals who were his own creation. He therefore reinstated God in the right place and dethroned the usurper who for the time being seemed to occupy the white throne. He emphasised and redeclared the central and unalterable existence of the moral government of this universe. He unhesitatingly said that the law was God himself. God's laws are eternal and unalterable and not separate from God Himself. It is an indispensable condition of his very preference. And hence, the great confusion that Buddha disbelieved in God and simply believed in the moral law."[28]

According to Gandhi, this is also not true that Buddha believed in the doctrine of no-soul (anātmavād). What the Buddha really disbelieved in was the soul as an eternal substance. In fact, the Buddha did not believe in anything eternal. According to him, change is the law of the universe and therefore everything is momentary. This is known as the doctrine of momentariness (kshanikavāda). What is called soul is nothing but a stream of passing moments of consciousness. And between any two moments of consciousness there is a necessary connection such that the first and the last moments of consciousness have an internal link. If this were not so, self-identity, memory etc could not be explained; end of all things Nirvana could have no meaning. If there were no soul, then who is bound and who gets nirvāna? The Buddha's answer is that although there is no permanent soul substance, the soul is not merely a sum total, a bundle (as Hume would say) of the moments of consciousness. It is rather a stream which implies that the moments are interlinked in such a way that the latter moments carry the samskāras of the previous moments. According to him the self is real, but is not an eternal substance. As a matter of fact the Buddha did not believe in the eternity of anything except Nirvāna.

The Buddha understood preached and practiced ahimsā in its true spirit. He felt that the teaching of ahimsā and the practice of the sacrifice of animals could not go together. So he regarded universal love and compassion as the real spirit of ahimsā. He did not attach importance to external practices, but lead much emphasis on the purity of motive. We should be non-violent not merely outwardly, but from the depth of our heart. We must not cherish any ill will or hatred towards anybody or any creature. We must always refrain from violence of all forms because violence solves no problem. Even the victory attained in a war is depreciated by the Buddha; Because according to him victory in a war involves violence and violence generates evil. He said, "Victory breeds hatred, for the conquered is unhappy."[29] He also said that we should not try to conquer wrath by wrath, rather we should conquer wrath by unwrath (akkhodhenajinekkhodham) According to him anger begets hatred and hatred is the source of all evil. Therefore, he always advised to refrain from anger, lust, hatred etc. and to practice *ahimsā* as the most celebrated virtue. This virtue is the first amongst the ten prescribed for the *samgha* and amongst the five rules of conduct (*panchashila*) prescribed for the layman.

To conclude, we may say that the Buddha taught a pure moralistic religion in which the eightfold path-the moral code of self-discipline played the most significant role. In place of a religion of rituals and sacrifices he gave a religion of high moral conduct. The Buddha perhaps never thought of founding a new religion. His aim, like Jesus, was only to reform. He was a Hindu and all who assembled around him were Hindus. But he came out as the founder of universal religion meant for all people, irrespective of caste, lineage or race. His message was universal and truly humanistic. His *sangh* contained people of all castes and from all walks of life. Also, his religion was a religion of self-dependence and self-help. Everybody could attain his highest goal by his own personal moral effort without the grace of any deity.

(D) ISLAM

Like other semitic religions, Islam is a prophetic religion, having for its prophet Mohammad. When Mohammad took birth in Arabia in the year 570 A. D., it was a land of polytheism full of various kinds of ritualism and idolatry. The religious life in Arabia in those days was really in a state of confusion. Against this, Mohammad preached a religion of strict monotheism and a life of rigorous ethical discipline devoid of any ritualism or idolatry. Amongst many attractive principles of Islam, two are very important (1) its unflinching monotheism, i.e., faith in only the God and no other (There is no God but Allah-La ilahaila' llahu) and (2) its unqualified submission (Islam) to God. On its ethical side, Islam teaches brotherhood of man and kindness, love and peace for all. Gandhi had a very high esteem for this religion and regarded it as a religion of love, peace and, above all, brotherhood of man. It is true that followers of Islam often took to sword for the spread of their religion, but this was not in accordance with the teaching of the Koran. As

Gandhi himself said in this connection, "I do regard Islam to be a religion of peace in the same sense as Christianity, Buddhism and Hinduism are. No doubt, there are differences in degree, but the object of all these religions is peace. I know the passages that can be quoted from Koran to the contrary. But so is it possible to quote passages from Vedas to the contrary... I have given my opinion that the followers of Islam are to free with the sword. But that is not due to the teaching of the Koran. That is due, in my opinion, to the environment in which Islam was born."[30] As a matter of fact, the common phrase used by Muslims for salutation, *Assalamalaikum*, means 'peace be on you', and this shows clearly that the religion of Islam in its true spirit is a religion of peace. The charge of fanaticism also sometimes levelled against Islam is not true. There are several passages in the Koran which speak of religious tolerance and thus the charge of fanaticism against it cannot be justified." Let there be no compulsion in religion; the right way is in itself distinct from the wrong."[31] Also, "But if thy Lord had pleased, verily all who are in the world have believed together. Wilt thou then compel men to become believers? No soul can believe but by the permission of God."[32] Gandhi said in this connection, "The prophet's whole life is a repudiation of compulsion in religion. No Mussalman has in my knowledge ever approved of compulsion. Islam would cease to be a world religion if it were to rely upon force for its propagation."[33] Of course, there is a definite place for what is known as *Jihad* in Islam and this *Jihad* is generally interpreted in terms of holy war against all those who are not the followers of Islamic faith." Fight those who believe not in God and in the last day, and who forbid not what God and His Apostle have forbidden, and who do not practice the religion of truth."[34] If this be taken as the real meaning of Jihad, then there seems to be a definite place for violence and compulsion in Islam and thus this religion cannot be saved from the charge of fanaticism. But there are differences of opinion and interpretation in respect of the exact implication of the provisions of Jihad in Islam. Let us see what Gandhi says in this connection, "My association with the noblest of Mussalmans has taught me to see that Islam has spread not by the power of the sword, but by the prayerful love of an unbroken line of its saints and fakirs. Warrant there is in Islam for drawing the sword, but the conditions laid down are so strict that they are not capable of being fulfilled by everybody. Where is the unerring general to order Jihad? Where is the suffering and love and purification that must precede the very idea of drawing the sword? We are too imperfect and impure and selfish, as yet, to resort to an armed conflict in the name of God."[35] This observation undoubtedly shows that there is a provision for Jihad, the holy war in Islam, but the conditions laid down for drawing the sword in the name of religion are so stringent that there can hardly be one entitled to resort to violence in the name of religion.

The tolerant and universalistic outlook of Islam can also be seen in its attitude towards other prophets and religions. It recognises the role and importance of all prophets such as Abraham, Moses, Jesus, etc. and takes all religions as the means for the spiritual upliftment of human beings. The Koran declares, "The same religion has been established for you that he enjoined on Noah, which we have by inspiration sent to thee. and that he enjoined on Abraham, Moses and Jesus, namely that you should remain steadfast in religion and make no divisions therein."[36] Furthermore, no divinity is ascribed to prophet Mohammad in Islam. He is simply regarded as the messanger (rasula) of God. This speaks of the simplicity and purity of Islam as a monotheistic religion. In this respect it is perhaps superior to Christianity in which Jesus, the founder prophet, is given the status of a God. And this contaminates the monotheistic character of Christianity.

All these aspects of Islam attracted Gandhi very much and he had every praise for the religion. His thoughts and ideas were very much influenced and moulded by the teachings of the Koran. No less than the teachings of the Koran was Gandhi influenced by the simple, austere, meek, humble and active life of the prophet Mohammad and his son-in-law Ali. C. F. Andrews has specially referred to the influences of these qualities of Mohammad on Gandhi. Gandhi himself has often referred in his writings to the early life of Muhammad, when he was despised and rejected by his own countrymen. Mohammad bore all sorts of humiliation in silence and with grace. Similarly, Gandhi had all praise for the long patient sufferings of the prophet's son-in-law Ali ant of Hassan and Hussain.

All these suffering according to Gandhi were the examples of non-violence and peaceful *satyāgraha*. He also found in the history of Islam the blending of the political with the religious and this perhaps reassured him in his faith that politics could not be separated from religion and that the political struggle required long and patient suffering.

Gandhi was also impressed by the social and personal codes of behaviour that Islam prescribes. In the Koran there are progressive codes of social behaviour and there is hardly any aspect of social life on which the Koran does not reflect and prescribe rules and regulations. There are regulations for marriage, divorce, dowry, inheritance, funeral ceremonies etc. The five pillars of Islam prescribe rules for personal behaviour. Prayer, fasting, alms-giving and hospitality are duties that every Muslim has to perform. All these influenced Mahatma Gandhi's thought and it is on account of these that he liked Islam very much. Furthermore, the Islamic ethics of the brotherhood of man and service to humanity impressed Gandhi a good deal. He found in Islam a firm base for real love and kindness for all. Gandhi found many of the injunctions of the discipline of Brahmacharya in Islam in the form of its prohibition of perfumed oil, intoxicating drinks, illegal sexual intercourse, etc. Virtues like obedience to parents, avoidance of adultery, cheating and lying, refraining from theft, murder etc. are also emphasized in Islam and all these influenced Gandhi in the formation of this code of ethical virtues.

(E) CHRISTIANITY

Amongst religions other than Hinduism perhaps no other religion inspired, impressed and influenced Gandhi so much as did Christianity. The teachings of Jesus have proved to be an important source of Gandhi's concept of *satyāgraha*. Basically, *satyāgraha* in the hands of Gandhi has been a weapon for conquering evil by good. This technique enables one to conquer his enemy by personal suffering and not by inflicting suffering upon the enemy. This lesson of *satyāgraha* Gandhi learnt mostly from the teachings of Jesus in the New Testament of the Bible. And this debt to the New Testament Gandhi has recognized himself. He has called Jesus the prince of *satyāgrahis*. In this connection we may very well refer to the following sermons of the Bible:-

"You have heard that it hath been said: An eye for an eye and a tooth for a tooth. But I say to you not to resist evil by evil: but if one strikes thee on thy right cheek. turn to him also the other.

"And if a man will contend with thee in judgement and take away thy coat, let go thy cloak also unto him. And whosoever will force thy one mile, go with him the other too.

"You have heard that it hath been said: Thou shalt love thy neighbour and hate thy enemy. But I say to you: Love your enemies, do good to them that hate you and pray for them that persecute and calumniate you.

That you may be the children of your father who is in heaven, who maketh his son to rise upon the good and the bad and raineth upon the just and the unjust.

For if you love them that love you, what reward shall you have? Do not even the publicans do this?

"And if you salute your brethren only, what do you more? Do not also the heathens do this?

"Be you therefore perfect, as also your heavenly Father is perfect."[37]

As we have already said, the Sermon on the Mount moved him most. He took this Sermon as the gift of Christianity and was so much impressed by it that he could very well bear the loss of his Gita. He said,

"What the Sermon describes in a graphic manner, the *Bhagavad-Gitā* reduces to a scientific formula.... Today supposing I was deprived of the *Gitā* and forgot all its contents, but had a copy of the Sermon, I should derive the same joy from it as I do from the *Gitā*."[38] The teachings of the Sermon on the Mount which Gandhi so much extolled and followed are as follows:-

"Blessed are the poor in spirit: for theirs is the kingdom of heaven.

Blessed are the meek: for they shall possess the land.

Blessed are they that mourn for they shall be comforted.

Blessed are they that hunger and thirst after justice for they shall have their fill.

Blessed are the merciful: for they shall obtain mercy.

Blessed are the clean of heart: for they shall see God.

Blessed are the peace-makers: for the shall be called the children of God.

Blessed are they that suffer persecution for justice sake: for theirs is the kingdom of heaven.

Blessed are ye when they shall revile you and persecute you and speak all that is evil against you, untruly, for man sake: Be glad and rejoice, for your reward is very great in heaven.

For so they persecuted the prophets that were before you."[39]

Gandhi loved Christianity much because of its absolute emphasis on love as the most important ethical virtue. As a matter of fact, it has identified love with God, the like of which no other religion has done. To quote Gandhi's own words in this connection,

"Christianity's particular contribution is that of active love. No other religion says so firmly that God is love and the New Testament is full of the word. Christians, however, as a whole have denied the principle with their wards."[40] Jesus taught and practised true *ahimsā* and true love. His whole life is an example of love and sacrifice for others. By courting his death at the Cross he faced the evil courageously and non-violently and with love and kindness for even those who were responsible for his crucifixion. The prayer of Jesus at the Cross is a superb example of meeting evil with love and non-violence-"Father forgive them, for they know not what they do." Gandhi was very much moved by this example. But he disliked the narrow way in which Christians generally interpreted this event of the Cross. He said, "The Cross undoubtedly makes a universal appeal the moment you give it a universal meaning, in place of the narrow one that is often heard at ordinary meetings; but then you have to have the eyes of the soul with which to contemplate it."[41] The Cross, rightly interpreted and understood in the true symbol of Christianity. It teaches not only retraining from hatred but overcoming evil and hatred by love and good will. Jesus on the Cross chose to meet evil unarmed and unafraid with love and good will for even those who were ready to kill him. And this indicates the true message of the Cross which Gandhi took to his heart.

But then Gandhi did not like the Christianity which many Christians followed and observed. He felt that Christianity as generally practised in the West was not loyal to the true spirit of the teachings of Jesus. Gandhi boldly asserted, "I consider western Christianity in its practical working a negation of Christ's Christianity. I cannot conceive Jesus, if he was living in the flesh in our midst, approving of modern Christian organizations, public-worship, or modern ministry."[42] And he said further, "The message of Jesus as I understood it is contained in his Sermon on the Mount, unadulterated and taken as a whole..... The message to my mind has suffered distortion in the West. It may be presumptuous for me to say so, but as a devotee of truth, I should not hesitate to say what I feel."[43] As a matter of fact, Gandhi saw in the religion of Christ a religion of deepest love for the whole of humanity, specially for the poor, meek and the humble, and an unambiguous and definite message of nonviolence and non-aggression even towards the enemy. But the Western Christians seem to have forgotten all these basic facts about Christ's teachings because they keep themselves engaged in violence, hatred and all such vices.

Gandhi also disliked the Christian dogma that Jesus was divine and that he was the only begotten son of God. In this connection he had every praise for Islam in which no divinity was ever claimed for Mohammad. He was simply regarded as a messanger of God. Gandhi said that if Christ was divine in nature, everybody could be taken as divine. All men are in a sense divine, and in that sense Christ also was divine. As Gandhi said, "If Jesus was like God, or God Himself, then all men were like God and could be God Himself.... I could accept Jesus as a martyr, an embodiment of sacrifice and a divine teacher, but not as the most perfect man ever born."[44] Against the claim that Christ was the only begotten son of God, Gandhi said, "I do not take as literally true the text that Jesus is the only-begotten son of God. God cannot be an exclusive father and I cannot ascribe exclusive divinity to Jesus: He is as divine as Krishna, Rama or Mohammad or Zoroaster. "[45]

Many Christians have so often claimed the superiority of Christianity over all other religions of the world. They believe that Christianity is the only true religion and that it is the fulfilment of all other religions. It is, so to say, the crown of religions and final redemption was possible only through it.

Gandhi was very much against such fanatic claims of Christianity. He was never ready to accept that Christianity was unique amongst religions and that it alone had the capacity to grant man his redemption. Gandhi asserted"..... there was nothing extraordinary in Christian principles. From the point of view of sacrifice, it seemed to me that Hindus greatly surpass Christians. It was impossible for me to regard Christianity as a perfect religion or the greatest of religions."[46] Gandhi, of course, recognised that Christianity was a noble religion, a true religion, but so were all the other religions of the world. There was nothing special about Christianity from the religious point of view. If Christianity could grant salvation to its people, all the other religions could very well do the same. Gandhi advised the Christians not to claim superiority for their own religion and to regard other religions as false or insufficient, but to be tolerant and sympathetic towards other religions. The Bible itself supports the claim that God has been equally good and kind to those also who have not held the Biblical faith: "Truly I perceive that God shows no partiality, but in every nation, any one who fears Him and does what is right is acceptable to Him."[47] Thus the Bible contains within it the gems of religious tolerance like the Koran and the other sacred texts of the different religions. Gandhi, however, felt satisfaction in the fact that the more reasonable amongst the Christians gradually began to realize the value of other religions also and showed signs of tolerance. He commended this growing spirt of tolerance. He believed that Christianity was really a great religion and one could learn much from it. But the Christians themselves must first be true Christians.

References

1. *Young India*, 6. 10. 1921.
2. *Ibid.* 29. 9. 1927.
3. *Ibid.*, 8. 4. 1926.
4. *Ibid.*, 6. 10. 1921.

5. *Rg. Veda*, X. 90.
6. S. Radhakrishnan, *Eastern Religions and Western Thought* (Oxford, 1939), p. 355.
7. *Young India*, 29. 1. 1925.
8. M. K. Gandhi, *In search of the Supreme*, edited by V. B. Kher (Ahmedabad, 1931), Vol. I, p. 230.
9. Paul Tillich, *Dynamics of Faith*, pp: 45-48.
10. *Harijan*, December 1936.
11. *Bhagavad-Gītā*, VI. 30. *Yo Mām pashyati sarvatra sarvam cha mayi pashayati, tasy hamānāpranashyām isa cha me nāpranashyati.*
12. S. Radhakrishnan. *op. cit.*, p. 21.
13. *Harijan*, 30. 1. 1937.
14. *Young India*, 11. 8. 1927.
15. *Ibid.*, 2. 9. 1926.
16. *Ibid.*, 29. 9. 1927.
17. *Ibid.*, 27. 8. 1925.
18. *Harijan*, Dec. 1936.
19. M. K. Gandhi, *All Men are Brothers*, edited by K. Kripalani, Unesco, 1958, p. 161.
20. *Ibid.*, p. 162.
21. Raghavan N. Iyer, *The Moral and Political Thought of Mahatma Gandhi*, p. 52.
22. Stephen N. Hay, 'Jain influence on Gandhi's early Thought' in S. Ray's (ed.), Gandhi, India and World (Univ. of California Press, 1970), p. 30.
23. *Ibid.*
24. *Young India*, 24. 11. 1927.
25. *Ibid*
26. *Dhammapada*, XXVI, 393.
27. *Dhammapada*, XXVI, 396.
28. *Young India*, 24. 11. 1927.
29. A. Coomarswary. *Buddha and the Gospel of Buddhism.* p. 17.
30. *Young India*, 10. 7. 1924.
31. *Koran*, II, 256.
32. *Ibid*, X, 99-100.

33. *Young India*, 29. 9. 1921.
34. *Koran*, IX, 29.
35. *Young India*, 10. 7. 1924.
36. *Koran*, XIII, 13.
37. *Matthew*, 38-48.
38. *Young India*, 31. 12. 1931.
39. *Matthew*, 2-12.
40. *Young India*, 31. 12. 1931.
41. M. K. Gandhi, *My Dear Child* (Navajivan, 1955), p. 86.
42. *Young India*, 23. 3. 1926.
43. *Ibid.*
44. M. K. Gandhi, *My Dear Child*, p. 170.
45. *Harijan*, March, 1937.
46. M. K. Gandhi, *op. cit.*, p. 170,
47. Acts, 10: 34-35.

❏

Chapter-II

Metaphysical and Religious Concepts

(A) MAN

Man has unveiled many mysteries, but has perhaps been unable so far in unveiling the mystery of his own nature. Great thinkers like Comte, Niebuhr, Sartre, Marx and many others have made attempts to understand human nature, but perhaps none of them has been able to understand it perfectly. However, broadly speaking, two kinds of attempts seem to have been made in the history of human thought to understand human nature. The one attempt has been to degrade it, to paint it in black colours, while the other has been to exalt and idealize it. Religions of the world, however, have, almost all of them, seen human nature in an exalted form. Hinduism has taken the soul within man as the divine spark within him. The Advaita doctrine takes human soul as identical with *Brahman*. The same divine soul is present in every human being according to it. The *Mahābhārata* says that there is nothing higher than man on earth-

Guhyam Brahman tadidam vo bravimi na mānusāt Sresthat-aram hi kincit.

Jainism holds that in the soul of man lies the potentialities of attaining infinitude or Godhood. Christianity tells us that man was made on the last day of creation and God made him in his own image. Man's creation on the last day signifies that man is the final fruit of creation had his being created in God's own image signifies his being essentially divine in nature. Similarly in Judaism, man's relationship to God is presented in the following verse:

He glories in me, He delights in me;

My crown of beauty, He shall be.
His glory rests on me, and mine on Him;
He is near to me, when I call on Him. (The Hymn of Glory)
The Islamic belief in the greatness of man is often expressed by the statement : *Khuda Ka noor usme hai.*

Gandhi's concept of man was formulated essentially in the light of such religious beliefs.

He took man's nature in a very exalted and idealized form. However, he did not completely ignore the animal aspect of human nature. He realized that man was a mixture of both animal and spiritual forces and therefore the presence of the animal traits in him could not be denied. Gandhi said, "Every one of us is a mixture of good and evil."[1] He believed in the theory of evolution and contended that before coming to his own species through the process of evolution, man belonged to the species through the process of evolution, man belonged to the species of the brute, and therefore brutal traits and dispositions have also been present in him. But the distinguishing mark of man is the spirit in him, which is really the divine spark within him. Man, of course, sometimes has a tendency to go downwards, but that is not his true nature. He said, "We were born with brute strength, but we were born in order to realize God who dwells in us. That indeed is the privilege of man and it distinguishes him from the lower animals."[2]

Gandhi was a deeply religious man and he took every man to be inherently religious. His concept of man was shaped by his deeply religious attitude which carried the impressions of the various religions of the world. But in formulating his concept of man, he seems to have been influenced most by his own religion, Hinduism. He had a deep respect for the Hindu Advaita, which, of course, he interpreted in his own way. His concept of man has a definite impression of this Advaitic faith. That can be well seen through the following summary of his views on the nature of man:

(1) All men are basically one, because in their souls they all share the same divine, the same Brahman. In other words, because the same Brahman resides in all of them, they are all equal.

(2) "If one man gains spiritually, the whole world gains with him and if one man falls, the whole world falls to that extent."[3] Thus

if one man is bad, that is not his long concern, rather it is the concern of all of us.

(3) What is possible for one man to achieve is possible for everyone to achieve. Because all men are equal, because the same divine spark is present in all of them, all are filled with similar potentialities and there is no reason why one man cannot achieve which the other can. What is required is equal effort and equal opportunity. The soul is one in all.

Its possibilities are therefore the same for everyone."[4]

(4) It is not desirable to possess ill will towards anyone or to speak ill of anyone. It is not also desirable to harm and injure anyone. Because there is the same divine residing in everyone, there is no sense in doing all these things to others.

(5) The service of society or the service of the whole of humanity becomes the duty of every man. We must think about every one and show love, sympathy and kindness to all because we are all basically one.

As Gandhi had firm faith in the essentially divine nature of man, he had also a firm faith in the essential goodness of man. All religious people believe that God is essentially good and because man is divine in his inner spirit he must also be essentially good. Gandhi, as we have already said, was a religious man out and out. Therefore he quite consistently believed in the essentially good nature of man. In this respect he fundamentally differed from the view points of such thinkers as Freud, Marx etc. He was also not very much appreciative of the Christian doctrine of the original sin, which characterized man as being tainted with sin and evil designs from his very origin. Gandhi believed that no man was ever inherently bad. Men, of course, sometimes perform evil deeds, but according to him, we must make a clear distinction between man and his deeds. There could be, and in fact there are, bad acts, but there are no bad men. Gandhi said, "Man and his deed are distinct things. Where a good deed should call forth approbation and a wicked deed disapprobation, the doer of the deed, whether good or wicked, always deserves respect or pity as the case may be."[5] This shows what a great respect and sympathy Gandhi had for man as such. There are only evil acts, no completely evil men who could not be reformed and changed. Gandhi firmly believed in the Buddhist theory of universal change and because, according to him, nothing was unchangeable human nature also was not inelastic and unchangeable. Man was essentially divine and good and therefore even those who apparently seemed to be the most devilish could be reformed by proper training and education. That man was teachable was a clear proof of the fact that he was essentially good. Gandhi always opposed the theory that man had essentially a degrading tendency and that he was always going downwards. He declared, "I refuse to believe that the tendency of human nature is always downward."[6] Of course, man according to him had an animal side also and that sometimes he had tendencies to go down, but that was not his essential nature and it was utterly false to say that the animal tendencies were predominant in him. The moment man is reminded of his true nature and is awakened to his true spirit, his animal side is subdued and he becomes a perfect man. Gandhi said, "Man's nature is not essentially evil; brute nature has been known to yield to the influence of love. You must never despair of human nature."[7] He had a firm belief in the spirituality as well as the rationality of man and he was confident that the rational and spiritual elements in him would never allow him to go down beyond a limit. He was very much optimistic about human nature and he believed that even the so-called worst man could be reformed and brought to the right track. "No human being is so bad as to be beyond redemption; no human being is so perfect as to warrant his destroying him whom he wrongly considers to be wholly evil. We must believe that every man can think for himself. The rationality of the human nature is the presupposition of human perfectivity."[8]

It was really on such optimistic beliefs about human nature that Gandhi built up his doctrine of satyāgraha and practised it throughout his life so consistently and confidently. His conception of *satyāgraha* rested on the belief and assumption that the innate goodness of even the most brutal of men could be aroused by the pure and undaunted suffering of a true *satyāgrahi*. Had he not believed in the innate goodness of man, he could not take the bold step of winning over even the worst of enemies by peaceful and non-violent means. He so confidently held the view that man was basically non-violent that he had not the least doubt in facing the worst of enemies non-violently. He said, "Man as animal is violent but as spirit (he) is non-violent. The moment he awakens to the spirit within he cannot remain violent."[9] He cautioned people against laying too much emphasis upon the evil nature of man. Man's essentially good nature was vitiated by the false and dangerous repetition of his evil nature. We should not therefore always highlight the evil nature of man. We should speak of the good in him and try to remove by training and sympathetic behaviour whatever evil traits might be found in him.

Gandhi was so optimistic about human nature that he believed that man was always going higher and higher both materially and spiritually. The gradual progress of civilisation from the state of cannibalism to the civilised life of agriculture etc. was, according to Gandhi, sign of progress towards ahimsā and love. Along with the change in everything, human nature was also changing and was changing for the better. All men were acting towards the realization of the inner, spiritual unity of mankind. As Gandhi affirmed, ".... the humans are working consciously or unconsciously towards the realization of that (spiritual) identity."[10] Gandhi was of the belief that one or two people might here or there due to wrong training or undesirable atmosphere behaved in unworthy ways, but mankind as a whole was working through the medium of love and *ahimsa*. Love was the true nature of man, because, as Christianity emphasized, love was the true nature of God, and man was essentially of the nature of God. Through the working of this law of love man was always going higher and higher. As Gandhi said, "I believe that the sum total of the energy of mankind is not to bring us down but to lift us up, and that is the result of the definite, if unconscious, working of the law of love."[11]Very few people have really such an optimistic picture of man in their hearts as Gandhi had, Gandhi not only had this picture but he also really worked on that with faith and conviction and achieved results. Some may argue against Gandhi that he had an unduly optimistic picture of man and he believed in the goodness of man more than what was necessary and desirable. But we are not so much concerned here with criticism of the Gandhian concept of man as with the elucidation and analysis of the concept. As to the criticism, however, this may be pointed out that opinions may well differ regarding the exact nature of man and everybody may not agree with Gandhi's view. But that hardly goes against Gandhi so long as he is loyal to his view throughout his writings, beliefs and practices. And that way Gandhi has been fully consistent. We have said above and will also mark in our references ahead that Gandhi's conception of *satyāgraha* was based essentially on his conception of man.

Gandhi, in the spirit of Jainism, believed in the infinite potentialities of man. According to the Jain view, human soul, although presently in the state of bondage. is in its real nature capable of attaining infinitude and perfection. Similarly, Gandhi believed that although in his present state man was imperfect, in the form of his soul he was divine and therefore he was inherently capable of attaining godhood or. perfection. In a different language, Tagore expressed the same belief by saying that man, though incomplete, was not imperfect. Perfection lies within him and he is able to realize that perfection by his own personal effort. Man's nature is progressive and he is always making efforts for the ideal of perfection. He may or may not attain the ideal, but he is always making efforts. Gandhi had firm faith in the power of the spirit that man had within him and he believed that this spirit of man had the capacity to change and reshape the course of events. "Life is an inspiration. Its mission is to strive after perfection, which is realization."[12] What was valuable for Gandhi was not the actual attainment of the ideal of perfection, but the efforts made for it by us. As he said, "Let us be sure of our ideal. We shall ever fail to realize it, but shall never cease to strive for it."[13] Perhaps no body was able to realize the ideal completely so long as he was under the limitations of the body. Being necessarily limited by the bounds of the flesh, we can attain perfection only after the dissolution of the body.

Gandhi was very confident about the power of man's soul-force. The soul within man had a potency, by virtue of which and by a proper cultivation of which man could do anything. He was fully capable of changing the society and the course of the universe. Here Gandhi was opposed to the total determinism of Marx, according to which the course of history was fully determined and no human effort could change it. Gandhi had a totally different conception of history. He believed that the soul force within man, which was really the force of love, could give history a different colour altogether. Criticising the Marxists, Gandhi said, "These people have concentrated their study on the depths of degradation to which human nature can descend. What use have they for the study of the heights to which human nature could rise?"[14]The Marxists had a very poor picture of man before them and they could not look into the depths of human nature in which there was a soul. The external brute force of man was based on egotism and all sorts of struggle and conflict were due to that. Marxists could see only this aspect of man. They missed the soul-force within which was the seat of love and which could create peace, harmony and happiness in society. Man was capable of achieving anything provided he could arouse the soul-force from within him. He could fight the worst of evil by his force of love within. Gandhi really reaffirmed here the position of Lord Buddha who taught that, " by rousing himself, by earnestness, by restraint and control, the wise man may make for himself an island which no flood can override." *(utthānenappam-ādena samyamena damena cha. Dipam kayirāth medhāvi yam odho nābhikarati)*[15]

It was due to his firm faith in the divinity of man's inner nature that Gandhi exalted human conscience and believed that there was no moral guide for the individual other' than his own conscience. And here Gandhi very much shared the view of Sri Aurobindo. He declared that the voice of man's conscience was the voice of God and one should follow the dictates of his conscience alone. It is reported that Gandhi himself always worked on the dictates of what he called the voice of his conscience. He so often reported experiences in which it appeared to him that someone was really speaking from within him and dictating him to adopt one particular course rather than another. This voice of conscience Gandhi could never ignore, because he believed it to be the voice of God himself. Gandhi lovingly termed this inner voice as' tyrant', the dictates of which he could not avoid. As the said, "The human voice could never reach the distance that is covered by the still small voice of conscience. The only tyrant I accept in this world is the still small voice within."[16] Gandhi's regard for the voice of conscience was further proof of his giving a very high place to individual person. But as there was fear of misuse of this doctrine of conscience by a few irresponsible and immature persons, Gandhi clearly defined what he meant by conscience and also who were the people competent enough to rely and work upon their con-science. He said, "Wilfulness is not conscience. A child has no conscience. The correspondent's cat does not go for the mouse in obedience to its conscience. It does so in obedience to its nature. Conscience is the ripe fruit of strict discipline. Irresponsible youngsters therefore who have never obeyed anything or anybody save their animal instinct have no conscience, nor therefore, have all grown-up people. The savages for instance have to all intents and purposes no conscience. Conscience can reside only in a delicately turned breast."[17]

Believing in the divinity and equality of all men, as well as in man's capacity for attaining perfection, Gandhi has always exhorted people to cultivate such moral virtues as *satya, ahimsa*, non-possession etc. and above all the service of humanity. Man being divine in nature is, no doubt, the crown of creation, but this does not imply that he is the master of the creation. According to Gandhi, he is rather the servant of creation and his duty is to serve the whole of creation.

Gandhi firmly believed in the law of *Karma*. Nevertheless, he believed in human free will also. According to Gandhi, as according to most of the Indian thinkers, the law of *Karma* does not contain within it a replica of determinism, rather it has ample scope within it for freedom of will. Law of *Karma* and freedom of will are not antithetical. The doctrine of *Karma* properly understood envisages that man is the maker of his own destiny, that everything about himself depends upon his own *Karmas*. No doubt, our previous *Karmas* limit to some extent our actions in our present life, but still there is ample scope for exercising our freedom for the construction of our future life. However, according to Gandhi, we are free only to act and not to produce results.

Results are in the hands of God. And here Gandhi seems to be fully under the impact of the *Bhagwad-gitā* according to which our right is only to act and not to control results. The results are beyond our control. We are free to strive for results, but it is not certain whether we would get the desired results. Our freedom, therefore, is not unfettered and unbounded.

Unlike Marx and others, Gandhi was an individualist who believed in the liberty of the individual person. He said that between the society and the individual, the latter was definitely more significant. Whenever Gandhi spoke of the greatness and the divinity of man, he always meant by that each individual man and not the collection of man. According to him, each individual contained within him infinite potency and immeasurable power and no power on earth could make the individual work against his will (contrast Schopenhauer according to whom the individual is nothing and less than nothing). About the strong individualistic bent of Gandhi Raghavan Iyer remarks, "It would not be extravagant to consider Gandhi as one of the most revolutionary of individualists and one of the most individualistic of revolutionaries in world history."[18] As a true votary of individual liberty Gandhi declared, "No society can possibly be built on a denial of individual freedom. It is contrary to the very nature of man. Just as a man will not grow horns or a tail, so will he not exist as man if he has no mind of his own. In reality even those who do not believe in the liberty of the individual believe in their own."[19] But again Gandhi did not minimize the importance of the society and believed that, because man was by nature a social being, the uplift of the individual was to a great extent bound up with the uplift of the society Therefore, he did not propound extreme individualism. He rather preferred a reconciliation between individualism and socialism. He said, "unrestricted individualism is the law of the beast of the jungle. We have learnt to strike the mean between individual freedom and social restraint. Willing submission to social restraint for the sake of the well-being of the whole society, enriches both the individual and the society of which he is a member."[20] However, of the two, viz., the individual and the society, Gandhi always gave the former a higher place and took the latter as nothing more than a mere aggregate of individuals. It was the society which existed for the individuals and not that the individuals existed for the society. In his views regarding the status of the individual in relation to the society and the State, Gandhi was very much influenced by the views of Rousseau. But above all, he was influenced by the supreme status given to individual men by such religions as Buddhism and Jainism. In this respect, Gandhi refused the Hegelian idea that the society and the State had a predetermined purpose superior to that of the individual and those individual ends were to be scarified on the altar of the social. He wanted every individual to be a 'full-blooded' individual and a fully developed member of the society. Against the Soviet social and political system in which the individual as an individual had hardly got any value, Gandhi often quoted the Bible, "What shall it avail man if he gains the whole world and loses his soul?" This clearly shows that Gandhi never wanted the individual soul to be subdued by the powers of the society or the State. However, Gandhi's individualism was based on Hindu concept of *dharma* according to which an individual had certain natural obligations towards the other members of the society.

The *Sādhārana* and the *varnāshrama dharmas* naturally bind the individual to the society in a kind of inevitable bond, in which each individual has to discharge certain obligations in relation to the other members of the society. Hence, according to Gandhi, the individual was not to be coerced for his obligations to the society, rather he was naturally to discharge certain obligations in accordance with his *dharma*.

It is the same kind of regard for individual liberty that seems to have guided Gandhi in his estimation of the relation between the individual and the state. He always looked towards the state, howsoever liberal it might be, with a suspicious eye. According to him, the state was there to assume more and more power to suppress individual freedom. He could not like the subjugation of the individual under the power of the state, because, according to him, while the individual had a divine soul within him, the state was a soulless machine. He regarded the state as a hindrance to individual liberty and moral progress. But because in practice it was not yet possible to dispense with the state totally, therefore in the spirit of Thoreau he so often said that that Government was the best which governed the least. He liked minimum of power to be assumed and exerted by the state over its citizens. He said, " I look upon the increase in the power of the state with greatest fear because, although while apparently doing good by minimizing exploitation, it does the greatest harm to mankind by destroying individuality, which is at the root of all progress."[21] This shows what a concern Gandhi had for individual liberty and freedom. At no cost he was ready to sacrifice that. He declared, "Submission to the state law is the price a citizen pays for his personal liberty. Submission, therefore, to a state wholly or largely unjust is an immoral barter for liberty."[22] He exhorted the individuals, therefore, not to obey laws of a tyrant or of an unjust State. He so clearly asserted in this respect, "You assist an administration most effectively by obeying its orders and decrees. An evil administration never deserves such allegiance. Allegiance to it means partaking of the evil. A good man will, therefore, resist an evil system of administration by his whole soul. Disobedience of the laws of an evil state is therefore a duty."[23] Like Kant, Gandhi believed that the individual alone was a moral entity, and therefore the state had no right to subdue his personality. What is most valuable is the individual man and so the interference of the State is just only to the extent to which individual freedom is not marred.

(B) GOD

It hardly needs repeating every time that Gandhi was a thoroughly religious man. Apparently, his whole life was political, but at bottom it was a religious life out and out. in fact, for Gandhi there was no absolute distinction between a political and a religious life. Politics without religion was, according to him, like a corpse without a soul. Religion sometimes goes without God also, but Gandhi as a religious man was a firm believer in God and, as he himself sometimes admitted, he could not live without God even for a moment. It is therefore necessary to see to some extent his own conception of God and the impacts of the various religious in the formation of this conception.

Gandhi was a staunch Hindu and his religious practices also more often seemed to be characteristically Hindu, but his conception of God is not a typical Hindu conception. It has impacts upon it of the religions like Christianity and Islam and also, peculiarly enough, of a religion like Buddhism which is so often regarded as a religion without God. But above all, Gandhi's conception of God is typically his own and is in a sense very radical and comprehensive. Of course, the overall impact of Hinduism cannot be denied.

Pre-eminently, Gandhi's conception of God seems to be one of a non-theistic nature. His God seems to be formless and impersonal like the God of the Hindu Advaitins. He used to characterize God as truth, goodness, life, living force, pure consciousness, the atheism of the atheists, and so on. Under the influence of Christianity, he so often characterized God as love and under the influence of Buddhism, as the Law or the *Dharma*. We remember him pleading against the characterization of Buddhism as atheistic. His theory was that Buddha never denied God, rather he identified God with His Law. The Law and the Law-giver become one in Buddhism according to him. He sometimes characterized God as the unseen, mysterious power pervading everything, the sum-total of all that exists, the indefinable and the indescribable power, the formless and the nameless. In our attempt to describe God we describe the indescribable, but God is really *neti, neti*–not this, not this. All these characterizations of God are very near to the Advaitic characterization of God as *Nirguna*, as an impersonal Absolute. Sometimes, Gandhi explicitly expressed his preference for the conception of God as a formless Truth. His characterization of God as Truth, which he emphasized very much, is also indicative of his preference for a conception of God as an impersonal Absolute. By 'Truth' or '*Satya*', he meant, as he himself said, '*Sat*' which in its turn meant 'Existence'. Hence by characterizing God as *Satya*, he perhaps wanted to take God as identical with the totality of existence, or with Existence as such, which again is an Advaitic conception.

But despite his preference for taking God as a formless Absolute, Gandhi never held inferior the concept of God as personal. He openly said that God was personal for those who needed a personal God. Under the influence of his Vaishnava background as well as due to the great impact that Christianity had made upon him, he sometimes characterized God as personal and gave him such attributes as omnipotence, omnipresence, omniscience, benevolence etc. Apparently, a contradiction may very well be smelt in the above two kinds of characterizations of God made by Gandhi. It is so often said that Gandhi was not a philosopher and therefore he did not understand the philosophical implications of his statements. Like an ordinary believer he took extracts from Hindu texts and tradition and so often uttered them without realizing their logical consequences. But the matter is not as bad as people have generally taken it to be.

Gandhi was certainly not a philosopher in the technical or academic sense of the term, but still he cannot be said to have been a victim of contradiction. He has been one of the most consistent thinkers and here also in his conception of God he has committed no logical error. Whatever he has said, he has said in the light of some of his basic convictions, which, if properly understood, leave no place for contradiction in his thought. For Gandhi God was above all a mystery, an indefinable power, a power beyond human grasp. Consequently, it was quite natural that human beings grasped his nature differently. Moreover, God was absolute truth which had got innumerable aspects. Human mind with its limitations was able to know only a few of them at a time with a relative stand-point. Under the influence of Jainism Gandhi was an *Anekāntavādin* and a *Syādvādin*, and therefore he had no difficulty in moving from impersonal to personal descriptions of God. He was an *Advaitin*, a *Dvaitin*, a *Vishishtādvain*—all at the same time but without any contradiction. It may be maintained, therefore, that Gandhi was fully aware of the implications of his personal–impersonal characterizations of God and he did it knowingly and consistently.

Some might argue that in characterizing God in personal-impersonal terms Gandhi was really distinguishing in the characteristic Advaitic fashion between the lower and the higher levels of reality. But this interpretation of Gandhi's thought would not also be faithful to his intention. He never took the two stands as higher and lower. Both the stands were equally important and valuable for him. From their own relative standpoints, both the stands were equally correct. Only for himself, Gandhi preferred taking God as formless Truth, as *nirākāra* and *nirguna*. As he clearly said, "I only prefer the worship of the formless. This preference is perhaps improper. One thing suits one man, another thing suits another man, and no comparison can fairly be made between the two."[24] Here again, one may have a clear indication of the tolerant and relativistic attitude of Gandhi. On the one hand Gandhi's conception of God as the all-pervasive, infinite, indefinable truth and on the other hand his relativistic attitude in matters of apprehending the nature of God made him go to the extent of saying about God that "He is all things to all men", meaning thereby that God had got so many facets that one could take him and describe him in any manner he liked. To have an idea of how Gandhi actually conceived God in his various facets, one may look to his following statement, "To me God is Truth and Love. God is Ethics and Morality. God is Fearlessness. God is the essence of light and Life and yet He is above and beyond all these. God is conscience, He is even the atheism of the atheist. For in His boundlessness, God permits the atheist to live. He is the searcher of hearts. He transcends speech and reason... He is a personal God to those who need His personal presence. He is embodied to those who need His touch. He is the purest essence. He simply is to those who have faith. He is all things to all men. He is in us and yet above and beyond us...."[25]

That Gandhi was not giving vent to a contradiction by his description of the nature of God as both impersonal and personal can be seen from a different angle also. Gandhi so often referred to God by such names as Rama, Krishna etc. and this was a clear example of his personification of God. But this was due to the impact upon him of the *vaishnava* tradition of his family. As a matter of fact, he realized within his heart of hearts that God could be given innumerable names, because really, he was nameless and formless. In his early youth, Gandhi relates, he was taught in accordance with the Hindu scriptures to repeat the thousand names of God, but he for himself. realized that the thousand names of God were not exhaustive and God could have many more names because he had many forms. As a matter of fact, he could best be regarded as nameless and formless. To quote his own words, "In my early youth I was taught to repeat what in Hindu scriptures are known as one thousand names of God. But these one thousand names of God were by no means exhaustive. We believe and I think it is the truth that God has as many names as there are creatures and therefore, we also say that God is nameless and since God has many forms we consider Him formless, and since he speaks to us in many tongues, we consider Him to be speechless and so on.....”[26] All the different names and forms given to the nameless and the formless were according to Gandhi various symbols with the help of which people made attempts to personalize what was impersonal and formless. As Gandhi said, “I have accepted all the names and forms attributed to God as symbols connoting one formless omnipresent Rama.”[27]

Thus, it is clear that Gandhi for himself took God as formless and the different personalized forms and names of God he considered as different symbols through which ordinary religious people made attempts to apprehend God and to establish living relationship with him. However, none of the two forms in which God could be apprehended was to be regarded as inferior or superior to the other. Both were equally valuable. Gandhi did not depreciate even the idol or image-worship. What he did not like, however, was to make a fetish of the idol. We have seen in our previous chapter in connection with his interpretation and understanding of Hinduism, that he took idol-worship as a practical means through which the ordinary man was able to pay his devotion to God and there was nothing wrong about it so long as the religious man was aware of the distinction between the idol and the real God. He expressed his real opinion about idol worship when he said, “Every Hindu child knows that the stone in the famous temple of Banaras is not Kashi Vishwanath. But he believes that the Lord of the Universe does reside specially in that stone.”[28] By saying that the Lord resided specially in the stone, Gandhi perhaps meant something like Paul Tillich that the stone in the Banaras temple being a symbol of the Lord, partook of the nature of the Lord, as all symbols do in relation to the reality which they symbolize. However, we may have the occasion to come to this point of comparison somewhat later on.

Gandhi believed in the absolute oneness of God, more or less, in the spirit of Islam. Of course, it does not mean that he took Hinduism as polytheistic. It simply means that he was very much impressed by the strict monotheism of Islam. He took Hinduism also as essentially monotheistic in nature. He admitted that the Hindus in practice worshipped many gods and goddesses, but then he emphasized that all Hindus knew it quite well that the different gods and goddesses were the various forms of the same formless Truth. They have been taught about this truth by the Vedas themselves: *Ekam Sadviprā vahudhāvadanti.*

Let us now come to the most important point in Gandhi's conception of God and that is his characterization of God as Truth. Gandhi considered the characterization of God as Truth to be the most appropriate. But to understand clearly the full implication of this characterisation let us first of all try to understand what truth actually means. In what sense did Gandhi take God as Truth?' Truth', ordinarily speaking, is taken as an attribute of our propositions and in this sense, it is a logical property. It is also used as an ethical virtue in the sense of truthfulness. But when Gandhi identified God with Truth beginning with a capital 'T' he was using the term in a very broad metaphysical sense in which, of course, these senses were also included. Truth in this broad metaphysical sense meant for Gandhi the abiding substratum which underlined everything. As he said, "This God whom we seek to realize is Truth. Or to put it another way, Truth is God. Thus Truth is not merely the truth which we are expected to speak. It is that which alone is, which constitutes the stuff of which all things are made, which subsists by virtue of its own power, which is not supported by anything else, but supports everything that exists."[29] There has been, in the Indian tradition, a belief that behind the flux of fleeting phenomena, there is a noumenal substratum which holds the entire universe and let it go on perpetually. Perhaps it is that noumenal substratum which Gandhi took as God and this is what he meant by '*Satya*'. This seems to be very clear from his following statesmen, "I do dimly perceive that while everything around me is everchanging, ever-dying, there is underlying all that change a living power that is changeless, that holds together, that creates, dissolves and recreates. That informing power or spirit is God. And since nothing else I see merely through the senses can or will persist, He alone is."[30]

This may be seen from a different angle also. Gandhi called God as Truth and sometimes he clearly said that by' Truth' or 'Satya' he meant 'Sat' or 'Existence'. And thus, by saying that God was Truth, he meant that whatever existed was God. In this sense God alone existed, because whatever existed was God and there was nothing other than God. Thus' Sat' in this sense was being taken as the sole underlying reality behind all existence. As Gandhi himself said, "The word Satya (Truth) is derived from Sat which means being. And nothing is or exists in reality except Truth."[31] Hence, because God or Truth in the sense of Sat includes entire existence, God or Truth alone really exists. In a different moment Gandhi depicted the same idea in this way, "Truth means existence, the existence of that we know and of that we do not know. The sum-total of all existence is absolute Truth or the Truth... That Truth I call God."[32] Here the word 'sum-total' may create a misunderstanding, but we must emphasize that the use of this inappropriate term is simply a result of Gandhi's not being well trained in technical philosophical terminology. His intention is quite clear from his statements quoted above. By' Existence' or 'Sat' he meant the all-abiding, all-pervasive basis which underlied all existence known or unknown. The same note of the all-comprehensive, all-pervasive and abiding nature of Truth is being depicted here. Hence Satya or Sat is that abiding, all-comprehensive, all-inclusive ground which holds and sustains everything.

The above might make it clear that one of the reasons behind Gandhi's emphasis on taking God as Truth was his intention to emphasize the absolute oneness of God. Truth in the sense of 'Sat' or Existence implies that whatever exists is God, that is, God alone exists and nothing else exists. This is very clear from Gandhi's own statement which he made by way of replying to a question as to why he took God as Truth, ".... And then we have another thing in Hindu philosophy, viz. God alone is and nothing else exists, and the same truth you find emphasized and exemplified in the Kalem of Islam. There you find it clearly stated—that God alone is and nothing else exists. In fact, the Sanskrit word for Truth is a word which literally means that which exists-Sat. For these and several other reasons that I can give you, I have come to the conclusion that the definition–Truth is God-gives me the greatest satisfaction."[33] This extract also shows the impact of both Hinduism and Islam in his formulation of the idea of God as Truth and in his emphasis upon the absolute oneness of God.

In Indian tradition 'Satya' has always stood for 'Abiding', 'Real' etc. and 'Mithyā' or 'Asatya' for 'fleeting', 'Apparent' etc. Moreover, 'Satya' has so often been identified with 'Dharma' or 'Ṛta'. These are all terms signifying or referring to something abiding which holds or sustains the entire existence. In the Vedic literature where Ṛta has been regarded as the natural and moral law sustaining the whole universe, 'Satya' is regarded as its essential nature or content. This shows that 'Satya' from the very early days has been regarded in Indian tradition as the abiding reality, as the fundamental law which holds the entire Universe. Gandhi also regarded Satya as entirely equivalent to Dharma. He declared that Dharma was the basis of all things and Satya was the basis of Dharma. It is in such senses taken together-metaphysical and moral both-that Gandhi used the term 'Truth' as synonymous with God and said that Truth was the most appropriate characterization of God or that Truth itself was God. Glyn Richards seems to be very right when he sees Gandhi's characterization of God as Truth in the following perspective, "Gandhi is faithful to the traditions of Hinduism when he affirms the isomorphism of Truth (Satya) and Reality (Sat). He refers to reality as Truth and by the use of the term he preserves the metaphysical and the ethical connection of such traditional Hindu terms as Dharma, Universal law or duty and Ṛta, the cosmic moral law. For him nothing is or nothing exists, except Truth...."[34]

Let us now try to see a few points regarding Gandhi's simple conversion of his statement 'God is Truth' to 'Truth is God'. Simple conversions of statements are logically prohibited. For example, it is not allowed by rules of conversion that the statement 'All men are mortal' be converted to the statement 'All mortals are men'. 'All men are mortal' can legitimately be converted to 'Some mortals are men'. But then there is an exception to this rule and that is that, when the denotations of the subject and the predicate of a statement are the same, simple conversions may be done. For example,

'All men are rational beings' might very well be simply converted into 'All rational beings are men'. In the light of this exception, Gandhi was very correct in making the simple conversion of his statement 'God is Truth' to 'Truth is God'. We have seen that according to him the only apt characterization of God is that he is Truth. 'Truth' as interpreted in the above sense has an identity of meaning for him with the term 'God' and therefore Gandhi, knowingly or unknowingly, committed no mistake in converting his former statement 'God is Truth' to 'Truth is God'. But the conversion was not merely a valid logical play for Gandhi. It had some definite purpose to serve for him. He very ably realized that so long as he used the term Truth as the predicate of the subject-term 'God', people might not properly understand the identity of meaning between the two terms that he wanted to convey. Being in the predicate, the term 'Truth' might only form one of the several predicates, such as love, kindness etc. attributable to God. But when it was transferred to the subject place and it was said that 'Truth is God', the identity between the terms 'Truth' and 'God' became quite clear. This made Gandhi's intention crystal-clear that he wanted to characterize God as Truth and Truth alone. Gandhi was a practical man also and not merely a theorist. Rather, we should say, he was a practical man out and out and not a theorist at all. And so, there were certain practical expedients too which made him do this kind of conversion. He wanted to bring even the atheists within this fold. But he felt that so long as he was characterizing God in the traditional way, the atheists might have a natural hesitation in coming within his fold. Therefore, he thought that if he characterized God as Truth and Truth alone then perhaps even the atheists could have no such hesitation. For, according to Gandhi, one could deny God, but nobody could deny Truth. Truth was the basis of everything for every one and even an atheist could not deny it. We don't know how far this argument is correct or how far Gandhi's interpretation of Truth would be acceptable to the atheists, but this is what he expediently believed when he rendered the above kind of conversion effective. Secondly, Gandhi regarded truth as the highest virtue but he felt that if he simply told people that it was the highest virtue, very few would take it seriously. Therefore, he hypostasized Truth by identifying it with God. As he himself said, "A mere mechanical adherence to truth and non-violence is likely to break down at the critical moment. Hence I have said that Truth is God."[35]

We can now summarise the main points involved in Gandhi's conception of God. God, according to him, is most essentially *Satya* or *Sat*, which means that he is Being or Existence as such. The various names and forms given to God are various symbols through which people try to establish living relationship with him. The various idols and images which people worship may also be taken as the various symbolic media through which they try to establish a correspondence with God. All these ideas contained in Gandhi's conception of God bear striking similarities with the ideas contained in Paul Tillich's conception of God. Gandhi was a simple religious man and Tillich a great theologian of modern times and therefore it may look somewhat surprising how the two agree in the essentials of their viewpoints regarding the nature of God. But, as will be evident from the considerations below, this is a fact. Of course, there are difference too, which is quite natural, but in their essentials the two seem to agree to a very great extent. Like Gandhi Tillich also takes God as Being. He says that 'God is Being-itself' is the only truth. Literal and non-symbolic characterization of God and all other statements about God are symbolic. Even the word 'God' is a symbol of Being-itself. All other characterizations of God as creator, all-powerful etc. are merely symbolic representations of his fundamental nature as Being-itself. About the nature of symbols, Tillich says that they point beyond themselves to what they stand for and they also partake of the reality they represent. [36]Gandhi also seems to have more or less similar ideas about symbols in his mind when he takes the personalisation of Truth as merely symbolic representations of it. Of course, he does not go into the detailed analysis of the nature of symbols and their exact religious significance as Tillich does.

According to both of them the various symbols through which Being or Truth is represented to men help him in establishing a living relationship with it. But there is a vital difference also between the two thinkers. While Tillich regards the personalised symbols to be of somewhat a lower status in comparison with the God as Being-itself, for Gandhi there is no question of lower and higher here. According to his *anekāntavāda* and *syādvāda*, even the personal characterizations of God in terms of various personalised symbols are equally good characterizations for those who require a personal God for their religious satisfaction. Gandhi disliked images or idols only when one made a fetish of them. So long as they are recognised as mere symbols there is nothing derogatory about them. Again, for Tillich, God is a mere symbol of the Being-itself which is the true religious or philosophical reality, but for Gandhi, although Truth or Being or *Sat* is the most apt characterization of God, God is not merely a symbol of Truth. The two are identical.

There is a further important similarity between Gandhi and Tillich in so far as both of them, in spite of their characterizing God as Being, take God as a Power or Force. Tillich very often characterizes God as Being-itself or the Power of Being.

This is clear from his statement, "...... instead of saying that God is first of all being-itself, it is possible to say that he is the power of being in everything and above everything, the infinite power of being."[37] Similarly, Gandhi also so often called God a power or force. Both of these thinkers perhaps realize that taking God as merely Being or *Sat* may reduce him to a mere unlively, static panorama standing behind the existence of the world, and that way he will be useless for religious purposes. Therefore, both of them take God as a Power. It is this power of Being or the force of Truth which enables everything to have the power to stand, or, to quote Tillich's words, to have the power of 'standing against non-being'. This conception of God as Power makes God lively and forceful. Thus, although Gandhi was not an academician, his conception of God has affinities with the conception of the same formulated by one of the greatest theologians of the modern world.

(C) RELIGION

Gandhi's concept of religion is very much in consonance with his concept of Truth or God. By 'Truth', we have seen, he meant, amongst other things, the Law, the Moral order, the *Dharma* or the *Ṛta*. It is in this sense that he very much liked the Buddhist idea of

God in which the Law and the Law-maker were one or the Law or the *Dharma* itself was God. Religion according to Gandhi is nothing but belief in this moral order.

To quote his own words, religion is "belief in the ordered moral government of the world."[38] But then religion is not merely a belief, according to him, it is a way of life also. He said, "You must watch my life, how I live, eat, sit, talk, behave in general. The sum total of all those in me is my religion."[39] Thus, religion is a specific way of life which can be visible in each and every dealing or behaviour of a man. It is neither a mere belief or faith nor it is a mere repetition of certain rituals on certain specific occasions. It gives a specific twist, a specific direction to one's entire life-pattern such that its impact is visible in every action. "Indeed, religion should pervade every one of our actions,"[40] said Gandhi. It is not merely an adherence to a particular sect. It is a pervasive pattern of life. Gandhi claimed himself to be a religious man out and out and his apparently political life was just an expression of his more pervasive religious life. That is, Gandhi's life was a truly religious life, because he had adopted a specific way of life and that way could be visible in every act that he performed or in every word that he spoke.

In taking religion as a pervasive way of life, Gandhi can be seen to be very near in his approach to some of the recent Western thinkers on philosophical theology, such as W. E. Kennick, Paul Schmidt and R. Braithwaite. These are all thinkers of the recent Western analytic tradition, but strangely enough through their analysis of religious language they reach the same conclusion regarding the nature of religion as that of Mahatma Gandhi. Religious statements, according to these thinkers in general, are expression of a pervasive behaviour pattern of the religious believer showing his intention to lead specific way of life. And this way of life concerns not only overt behaviour, but also inner dispositions, i.e., the way of feeling and thinking also. By taking religion as a way of life, these thinkers want to point out that religion is very near to morality and that morality constitutes the very essence of religion. Braithwaite is most vocal of all these thinkers in comparing religion to morality. Taking the example of Christianity, he says that being a Christian really means nothing but leading or having an intention to lead an agapeistic way of life, i.e., a life of love. And hence, religion in its essence is nothing but morality. Gandhi also quite in tune with the view of these thinkers took religion as very intimately related to morality; rather he took morality to be the essence of religion. In this respect, he seems very much influenced by Buddhism as a religion. In the words of Gandhi "True religion and true morality are inseparably bound up with each other. Religion is to morality what water is to the seed that is sown in the soil."[41] Or again, "As soon as we lose the moral basis, we cease to be religious. There is no such thing as religion overriding morality. Man, for instance, cannot be untruthful, cruel and incontinent and claim to have God on his side."[42] Thus morality, according to Gandhi, forms the essence of religion. True religion changes our nature, purifies our character. Whitehead also took religion, at least of its practical side, to be very intimately related to our character. He said, "A religion, on its doctrinal side, can thus be defined as a system of general truths which have the effect of transforming character when they are sincerely held and vividly apprehended."[43] Similarly, Gandhi held religion to be that "which changes one's over nature, which binds one indissolubly to the truth within and whichever purifies:"[44] Of all the moral virtues, however, which constituted the essence of religion, Gandhi quite naturally took truth to be the highest. He sometimes even identified religion with truth and righteousness. As he clearly said, "There is no religion higher than Truth and Righteousness."[45] And here Gandhi was in a way echoing the old Vedic faith that truth constituted the essence of the all-pervasive moral principle of *Ṛta*. We have seen that religion in a very general sense meant for Gandhi the all-pervasive *Dharma* or *Ṛta* and because truth was taken to constitute the essence of *Dharma* or *Ṛta*, naturally Truth constituted the highest religion for him.

But in spite of the fact that Gandhi, like many Western thinkers, took religion as a way of life, as a moral way of life rather, and above all, a life of truth and righteousness-he also very significantly differed from them in his own concept of religion. He did not take religion as a way of life in a cut-and-dry sense. The way of life which constituted religion must be rooted, according to him, in a faith or conviction in God or Truth. We have seen that 'God', according to him, did not necessarily mean a personal God. It rather meant for him the permanent spiritual and moral basis behind the universe which had its spark in man also in the form of his soul. Religion was, according to Gandhi, a way of life directed and regulated by a faith in God in this sense. Thus, religion was not simply a way of life, rather it was a way of life based on the spiritual conviction that the world was sustained by Truth, by *Dharma* and that there was an ordered moral and spiritual basis behind it. It is really this conviction which supplied Gandhi with a firm foundation for the way of life that he practically led. Religion for Gandhi thus was a way of life based on some specific spiritual conviction with regard to the universe as a whole.

There is another important aspect of Gandhi's concept of religion which also seems to be most influenced by the Buddhist ideas, although impact of religions such as Hinduism, Christianity, Islam etc. may not be ruled out. Whitehead said about religion that it was something 'which the individual does with his solitariness'. But it seems that Gandhi did not much approve of this individualistic and private character of religion. According to him religion was not something which concerned a man in his isolation from his fellow beings. True religion consisted in helping the helpless and the poor and working for the welfare of humanity, or rather of the entire creation. God was everywhere and in everything. But he resided specially in the poor and the helpless. Therefore, serving the poor was the greatest form of religion according to Gandhi. He used to say, "I am endeavouring to see God through the service of humanity, for I know that God is neither in heaven nor down below, but in everyone."[46] Such statements clearly show that Gandhi fully recognised the theonomous character of humanitarian activities. He was very much captured by the Christian sermon 'Love your neighbour as yourself'. Religion consists in nothing but loving one's neighbour as oneself, and for that matter, loving the entire humanity and entire creation. All religions invariably teach this lesson of love and brotherhood, but Christianity teaches this lesson in the most effective manner by identifying God with Love. It is again Christianity which teaches service of the poor and the needy. All these had definite impact upon Gandhi and consequently he took religion primarily as consisting of love, kindness and sympathy towards others.

Gandhi's conception of religion as a way of life based on some sort of spiritualistic conviction with regard to the universe as a whole may be seen to be equally applicable to all the prevalent religions of the world. Religion, whether it be Hindu, Buddhist, Jain, Christian or any other, consists of certain specified principles of living as well as of certain beliefs or convictions which govern, guide or direct such principles of living. Gandhi, therefore, regarded all the different religions as different roads leading to the same goal. This goal is the goal of Truth which the different religions conceive or apprehended in their own relative ways. Truth is the basic reality which every religion tries to apprehend in its own way. The specific conviction of every religion in regard to the universe as a whole may be interpreted in the light of Gandhi's views as its specific vision of Truth. Truth in itself is one and absolute, but our glimpses of it are relative and many. Here again Gandhi seems influenced by the *anekāntavāda* and *sayādvāda* of Jainism. Truth has many facets and we as finite human beings are able to apprehend some or other aspect of it only relatively. All the different religions are different attempts at apprehending the absolute Truth in partial and relative ways. All religions, therefore, are bound to be imperfect, because all of them interpret Truth only partially in their own ways. But it is not that some religion is more imperfect and other less imperfect or that someone is imperfect and the other is perfect. Such distinctions are quite arbitrary. All religions are imperfect, but again all are valuable in their own ways in as much as all of them provide ways to their followers to realize the ultimate or absolute Truth. It matters little, therefore, which road one adopts to realise Truth. Each one is free to adopt that road which suits his environment and temperament. As Gandhi himself said in this connection, " Religions are different roads converging to the same point. What does it matter that we take different roads, so long as we reach the same goal? In reality, there are as many religions as there are individuals."[47] Here Gandhi was more or less echoing the idea of the great neo-Vedantist Vivekanand who also took different religions as representing the different aspects of the same Truth partially, and which could therefore be regarded as different paths leading to the same goal.

Here in a part of the above statement of Gandhi, viz. in 'what does it matter that we take different roads, so long as we reach the same goal?', one may very well mark a discrepancy in his thought. Gandhi usually said that the end could not justify the means, but here it seems that he was trying to justify the means with reference to the end. The path did not matter, he said, if the goal reached was the same. Thus, here it seems Gandhi was going back from his stand and was trying to impress that so long as the goal of Truth was achieved, means, whatever they might be, did not matter. But taking Gandhi here in this light would simply be to misunderstand and misinterpret him. It must be kept in mind that when Gandhi was counselling to adopt any religion as a path to the goal of Truth, he had in his mind his firm conviction that all religions, though imperfect, were nevertheless equally valuable and there was no question of superiority or inferiority amongst them. Because as all religions were equally valuable, there was no harm in adopting any one of them as means to the realization of Truth. Thus, what Gandhi was really suggesting by his above statement was that no undue importance should be given to any particular religion in preference to others.

The above remarks of Gandhi regarding the status of various religions amply show that he was averse to calling any particular religion as superior or inferior to any other religion. According to Gandhi all the religions had imperfections because all of them revealed only partial and relative truths, but again all were equally holy because all were the creations of the same God. His view will be clear from his own statements that follow, "... if we are imperfect ourselves, religion as conceived by us must also be imperfect. We have not realized religion in its perfection, even as we have not realized God. Religion of our conception, being thus imperfect, is always subject to a process of evolution and reinterpretation.... And if all faiths outlined by men are imperfect, the question of comparative merit does not arise. All faiths constitute a revelation of Truth, but all are imperfect and liable to error."[48] Again, "God has created different faiths, just as He has the votaries thereof. How can I even secretly harbour the thought that my neighbour's faith is inferior to mine......? In God's house there are many mansions and they are equally holy."[49] For himself, Gandhi possessed a true respect for all the religions of the world and enjoined upon others to keep a similar attitude towards the faiths of others, because all of them contained an element of truth. Gandhi, in short, preached an attitude of what he called tolerance towards other religions. He did not, as he himself said, liked the word' tolerance', because it had a sense of uneasy toleration behind it and it might imply within it the "gratuitous assumption of the inferiority of other faiths to one's own." But for want of a better word, Gandhi used it in the sense of not only toleration, but also in the sense of positive love, respect and regard for other religions. Different religions were different interpretations of the same truth and it was not possible to decide conclusively which interpretation was correct. Hence the necessity of religious tolerance. To quote Gandhi himself in this connection, "Even as a tree has a single trunk, but many branches, so there is one true and perfect Religion, but it becomes many, as it passes through the human medium. The one Religion is beyond all speech. Imperfect men put it into such language as they can command and their words are interpreted by other men equally imperfectly. Whose interpretation is to be the right one? Everybody is right from his own standpoint, but it is not possible that everybody is wrong. Hence the necessity of tolerance, which does not mean indifference to one's own faith, but a more intelligent and purer love for it. Tolerance gives us spiritual insight, which is as far from fanaticism as the north pole from the south. True knowledge of religion breaks down the barriers between faith and faith."[50]Like a true student of Comparative Religion, Gandhi advised people to read others' religions sympathetically through the writings of such persons who were ardent votaries of those religions. That would increase one's understanding of other religions as well as of the inner unity of all religions depicting the same truth. "There is one rule, however, which should always be kept in mind while studying all great religions and that is that one should study them only through the writings of the known votaries of the respective religions...... This study of other religions besides one's own will give one a grasp of the rock-bottom unity of all religions and afford a glimpse also of the universal and absolute truth which lies beyond the 'dust of creeds and faiths'."[51] He flatly rejected as mistaken the notion that the sympathetic study of other religions might weaken a believer's faith in his own religion. He was of the view that on the contrary such a study might well strengthen one's regard for one's own religion along with others. As he declared, "Let no one even for a moment entertain the fear that a reverent study of other religions is likely to weaken or shake one's faith in one's own. The Hindu system of Philosophy regards all religions as containing the elements of truth in them and enjoins an attitude of respect and reverence towards them all. This, of course, presupposes regard for one's own religion. Study and appreciation of other religions need not cause a weakening of that regard; it should mean extension of that regard to other religions."[52]

As a natural corollary to his sense of equal respect for all religions, Gandhi did not approve of the idea of conversion, specially through such dubious means as those of coercion and material inducement. He was thus very much critical of the Christian missionaries which were engaged in converting poor Hindus to Christianity by means of material inducements. This was really a trade or business of religion according to him. When all religions were of equal value, and a man was finding spiritual satisfaction through his own religion, what was the need of converting him from his own faith to some other? The effort at converting people by Christian missionaries was really a replica of the false notion of the many Christians that Christianity was the most superior of all religions and that it was best able to save the souls of people. We have seen that Gandhi was totally averse to such notions of superiority and inferiority in matters of religion. He could not even cherish the idea in his mind that somebody should be converted to his own religion. As he said, "How can I even secretly harbour the thought that my neighbour's faith is inferior to mine and wish that he should give up his faith and embrace mine? As a true and loyal friend, I can only wish and pray that he may live and grow perfect in his own faith."[53] The aim of every one of us should be, according to Gandhi "to help a Hindu to be a better Hindu, a Mussalman to become a better Mussalman, and a Christian a better Christian"[54] and not to convert people of other faith to our own religion. That is really a useless and in a sense illusory effort. Gandhi wrote to a correspondent, who advised him to save his soul by conversion to Christianity in the following words "God is not encased in a safe to be approached only through a little hole in it, but He is open to be approached through billions of openings by those who are humble and pure of heart."[55]

However, it would be wrong to conclude on the basis of the above that Gandhi was averse to conversion as such. He was really opposed to conversions which were forced or which were attempted through material inducements. He was not opposed to voluntary conversions. In an important sense one's religion was for him a personal matter and it was for him to decide and see which particular religion gave him the best spiritual satisfaction. But for that no dubious methods need be employed. A religion by its spiritual commitments was able enough to attract people in its fold, if it possessed certain special things for the religious man. For that no coercion or undue inducement was required. In almost a poetic vein Gandhi said in this connection, "A rose does not need to preach. It simply spreads its fragrance. The fragrance is its own sermon.... The fragrance of spiritual and religious life is much finer and subtler than that of the rose."[56]That is, if a religion had certain special qualities, certain attractions for a man, he would be naturally drawn towards it. Conversion is a matter of heart and therefore by merely converting the label of a man, real religious conversion could not be brought about. Gandhi was so much critical of the missionary activities of the Christians that he once said that if Jesus came to the world once again, he would like to own some of the non-Christians more than such Christians who had forgotten the real message of Christ and were engaged in totally unchristian activities. As he said, "..... many men who have never heard the name of Jesus Christ or have even rejected the official interpretation of Christianity would probably, if Jesus came in our midst today, be owned by him more than many of us."[57] In this regard Gandhi was very much appreciative of the attitude of Hinduism and Jainism. Hinduism has always been quite liberal and tolerant towards other religions and its philosophy has been to regard all religions as true and valuable in their own ways.

When Gandhi was speaking of the partial but equal status of all religions, it was really this Hindu spirit that was finding echo through him. Further, the Jain *Syādvāda,* i.e., the theory of the relativity of truth, filled him with the conviction that all religions expressed the same Truth relatively and therefore all were correct in their own ways. There was no question of superiority or inferiority there. Gandhi was no less influenced in this respect by the several references in the Koran which spoke of religious tolerance.

So far, things have been rather very plain in Gandhi's concept of religion and his attitude towards other religions. But there may be seen in his views at certain places, attempts to mystify or hypostasize religion. It seems at places that by religion he meant that essence, that common denominator, which underlie all the different prevalent religions. So far as he says that there is one basic absolute Truth which is revealed in relative ways through the different religions and that the different religions are all ways towards the same Truth, things are understandable. But, according to him, there is not only the Absolute Truth but also the Absolute Religion, so to say, which is only partly expressed through the different religions. Different religions are but the incomplete, partial manifestations of the one basic Religion which is beyond all speech. This may be seen through his own statement, "By religion I do not mean formal religion or customary religion, but that Religion which underlies all religions."[58] His other statement, we have already quoted above in another reference, but a portion of that we are quoting again to testify the point at hand, "Even as a tree has a single trunk, but many branches and leaves, so there is one true and perfect Religion, but it becomes many, as it passes through the human medium. The one Religion is beyond all speech."[59] Now it is not precisely clear what Gandhi meant by this one basic true and perfect Religion, which according to him, underlie all particular religions. Did he believe that something like a primordial essence underlie all the different particular religions which could be taken as the true religion? If yes, then in this sense true religion must become a primordial entity of which different religions became partial manifestations. Gandhi sometimes seems talking in that vein and therefore one has every reason to doubt whether he was hypostasizing religion while he was designating it with a capital 'R. We have seen Gandhi saying that no particular religion could embody the basic Religion in its absoluteness and therefore each one of them was incomplete and erroneous. Again, we have found him saying that each particular religion contained some element of the true Religion and that the true primordial Religion found concrete expression only in and through those particular religions.

In our opinion, there is little likelihood that Gandhi was hypostasizing religion when he used the word 'Religion' with a capital 'R' to denote the true and fundamental religion. He may, however, be taken as mystifying religion to some extent because he sometimes seems giving religion an identical status with the mysterious reality God or Truth. It may be said that in a fit of emotion Gandhi sometimes used the word 'Religion' for 'Truth' itself. When he said that behind and beneath a particular religion, there underlie the one true Religion, he actually meant the Truth or God himself which underlie all the religions as the basic Truth. This may be a correct interpretation, but we have from our side a deeper meaning to suggest in this connection.

We feel that Gandhi's use of the word 'Religion' with a capital 'R' was not merely emotive or accidental, rather it had some viable sense to carry and that sense fits in with his general conception of religion that we have outlined in the early pages of this topic. By 'Religion' he did not mean Truth, rather he meant by it the vision of the Truth. And by Truth, we know he meant the underlying basis of all things, the permanent substratum behind the passing flux of phenomena. Perhaps he was echoing here the following words of Whitehead: "Religion is the vision of something which stands beyond, behind and beneath the passing flux of immediate things,.. something which is the ultimate ideal, and the hopeless quest."[60]This vision really works as an ideal which regulates our behaviour and activities in the world in a specific way. The fundamental Religion is this fundamental vision which different religions take in different ways. According to Gandhi, we have seen, religion is a way of life based on some conviction or vision with regard to the universe as a whole. The vison interpreted differently in different religions gives vent to different ways of life. The vision, as we have said, serves as an ideal which regulates the life of the religious man. The fundamental vision or the fundamental ideal which is something of its own unique nature, finds partial expressions in the form of various religions and the consequent various ways of life. Religion in the Gandhian sense is fundamentally this vision, which due to its unique nature is really speechless. Human beings give language to it in accordance with their own capacities. As Gandhi has said, "The one Religion is beyond all speech. Imperfect men put it into such language as they can command...."[61]

Thus, it seems to us that Gandhi had a deeply significant sense to convey about the fundamental nature of religion when he spoke of Religion with a capital 'R'. We have said above that religion according to Gandhi was not a matter of private affair. It consisted rather in one's discharging the essential moral responsibilities towards one's fellow beings. But this is only the practical side of the religion of Gandhi's conception. It has besides a more fundamental side too in respect of which it could be taken as individualistic and private. The fundamental vision which is the mother of all prevalent religions occurs to an individual only when he is in a state of meditative solitariness. Religion is fundamentally a vision and it is in the nature of that fundamental or primordial vision that religion is one. It is this fundamental religion which Gandhi designated as the Religion with a capital 'R'. On the practical side, there are many religions giving vent to the different ways of life, but fundamentally Religion is one.

References

1. *Harijan*, June, 1939.
2. *Harijan*, April. 1938.
3. *Young India,* December, 1924.
4. *Harijan*, May, 1940.
5. M. K. Gandhi, *The Story of My Experiments with Truth* (Navajivan, 1956), p. 276.
6. *Young India,* Dec., 1926.
7. *Harijan,* November, 1938.
8. *Young India*, March, 1931.

9. *Harijan*, August, 1940.
10. Gandhi's Correspondence with Government, p. 82.
11. *Young India,* November, 1931.
12. *Harijan*, June, 1935.
13. Speeches and Writings, p. 301.
14. S. Nayyar, *Bapu ki Kārāvās ki Kahāni*, p. 152.
15. *Dhammapada*, II, 5.
16. *Young India*, March, 1922.
17. *Ibid.*
18. Raghavan Iyer, *op. cit.,* p. 114.
19. *Harijan*, February, 1942.
20. *Harijan*, May, 1939.
21. *Modern Review*, October, 1935.
22. *Young India*, January, 1927.
23. P. Sitaramayya, *The History of the Indian National Congress* (Padma Publication, 1946), Vol. I, p. 649.
24. *Diary of Mahadeve Desai* (Navjivan, 1953), Vol. I, p. 168.
25. *Young India*, 5. 3. 1925.
26. *Young India*, 31. 12. 31.
27. M. K. Gandhi, *In Search of the Supreme*, compiled by V. B. Kher (Navjivan. 1931), Vol. I, p. 214.
28. *Ibid,* p. 230.
29. *In Search of the Supreme*, Vol. I, p. 196.
30. *Young India*, 11. 10. 1928.
31. *Yeravda Mandir*, p. 1.
32. Gora, *An Atheist with Gandhi* (Navjivan, 1951), p. 48.
33. *Young India*, 31. 12. 1931.
34. Glyn Richards, *The Philosophy of Gandhi* (Curzon Press London, 1982), p. 1.
35. *Harijan*, July, 1947.
36. Paul Tillich, *Systematic Theology*, Vol. I, pp. 235-42; Also his Dynamics of Faith (Harper & Row, N. Y., 1958), pp. 45-48.
37. Paul Tillich, *Systematic Theology*, Vol. I, p. 236.
38. *Harijan*, Feb., 1940.
39. *Ibid,* Sept., 1946.
40. *Ibid.*
41. M. K. Gandhi, *Ethical Religion* (Madras, 1930), p. 49.

42. *Young India*, 24. 11. 1921
43. A. N. Whitehead, *Religion in the Making* (Macmillan, 1926), a portion of which is included in Abernethy and Langford (ed.) *Philosophy of Religion* (Macmillan, 1958). The Lines quoted are from this book, p. 50.
44. *Young India*, May, 1920.
45. *Ethical Religion*, p. 49.
46. Louis Fischer (ed.) *The Essential Gandhi* (New York, 1962), p. 229
47. *Hind Swaraj* (Nov., 1944), p. 24.
48. *Yeravda Mandir*, p. 55.
49. *Harijan*, April, 1934.
50. *Yeravda Mandir*, p. 55.
51. *Young India*, Dec. 1928.
52. *Ibid.*
53. *Harijan*, April, 1934.
54. N. R. Bose, *Selections from Gandhi*, p. 259.
55. *The Diary of Mahadeva Desai*, Vol. I, Entry Sept. 4, 1932.
56. *In Search of the Supreme*, Vol. 3, p. 83.
57. *The Essential Gandhi*, p. 234.
58. J. J. Doke, *M. K. Gandhi* (Natesan, 1909), p. 7.
59. *Yeravda Mandir*, p. 55.
60. A.N.Whitehead, *Science and the Modern World* (Macmillan), New York, 1926), P. 191.
61. *Yeravda Mandir*, p. 55.

❑

Chapter-III

Social and Political Concepts

(A) TRUTH

Truth *(Satya)* and non-violence *(ahimsā)* are the twin concepts which seem fundamental to the whole of Gandhi's social and political philosophy. Of course, Gandhi is more known to the world for his concept and practice of non-violence than anything else, but he himself took the concept of truth as more fundamental and more important than that of non-violence. This is very clear from his own statement that he once made, "As a Jain *muni* once rightly said, I was not so much a votary of *ahimsā* as I was of truth, and I put the latter in the first place and the former in the second. For, as he put it, I was capable of sacrificing non-violence for the shake of truth. In fact, it was in the course of my pursuit of truth that I discovered non-violence."[1] Gandhi took a*himsā* merely as a means and truth as a goal.

Let us see, therefore, at some length what Gandhi actually meant by truth and how far he has been influenced by religion or religions in the formation of the concept of truth. 'Truth' or '*Satya*' is generally used in two senses—logical and moral. In its logical sense, it is used in the sense of the logical value of propositions such as 'Ram is ill' is true or 'Ram has gone to Delhi' is false. Here 'true' and 'false' are the logical valuation of the propositions to which they have been ascribed. Such propositions are simple statements of fact having no sense of 'good' or 'bad', 'right' or 'wrong' attached to them. But there is a sense in which 'truth' is regarded as a great moral virtue and it is advised as an important moral percept that one should always speak the truth and never adopt falsehood. Gandhi has used the term 'Truth' in this sense of moral virtue. According to him, truth or *Satya* is the greatest moral virtue *(satyam nāstiparodharmh)*. In this sense truth seems truthfulness, that is, speaking the truth. Speaking the truth means speaking whatever is true to facts. Sometimes it also means speaking whatever is just, that is, valid in the eyes of justice. 'Falsehood' is the opposite of truth. But simply speaking what is not true to fact is not falsehood. Distorting the truth or hiding the truth or keeping silent about the truth is also falsehood. And just as truth is the greatest virtue, falsehood is the greatest vice or sin. Gandhi always advised to speak the truth and stand firmly in support of the path of truth and justice. Truth for Gandhi was an absolute value. It was never to be compromised. Of course, this sustenance to truth in a firm manner required courage and fearlessness. And for these, complete selflessness and non-attraction towards worldly possession were necessary. Without being fearless one can't speak the naked truth and also so long as one has selfish motives and has many stakes for personal gain he can neither have the courage to speak the truth himself nor can he support others in exposing falsehood. Only a man with a selfless motive who has nothing to gain or lose for himself can be fearless enough to speak the truth. In short, *aparigrah* is necessary for *abhay* and *abhay* is necessary for speaking what is *Satya*.

There is a Sanskrit verse which Gandhi so often repeated *Satyam bruyāt, nabruyātsatyamapriyam*. The verse is generally taken to mean that one should speak the truth, but not that truth which is unpalatable to the listener. But the virtue of truth-speaking will be meaningless, if the word is taken in this sense. For, truth will always taste unpalatable to a listener, who is a wrong-doer. So if we always care whether the truth that we are going to speak will taste good to the listener or not, then most of the wrongs will remain unexposed and injustice will be done for want of truth being brought to the forefront. So Gandhi takes the word in his own way to mean that one should speak the truth, but not in a harsh language. It should be spoken in a sweet and polite language. This meaning of the word was quite in keeping with Gandhi's views about *ahimsā*. According to Gandhi *ahimsā* in its broad sense meant not hurting anyone in any way that is, neither in thought, nor by words, nor by deed. So if truth is spoken in polite and sweet language it will not hurt the listener at least in one way. He will, of course, be hurt in another way, if he is a wrongdoer because by speaking the truth the speaker will expose his falsehood or wrongdoing but that can' t be helped. If we want to bring out truth to the forefront so as to uphold truth as the greatest virtue. If we take the verse in the first sense or in the general sense, then it will be more or less, impossible to speak the truth, because its speaking the truth will always be unpalatable to the wrong doer.

We have said above that for Gandhi truth was an absolute value and therefore there could be no compromise in matters of truth on this or that plea. As a general rule, truth must be spoken in any case. But because as human beings we are bound under certain limitations, circumstances sometimes compel us to hide the truth or speak otherwise. For example to save the life of an innocent person sometimes, we have to hide the truth or take recourse to falsehood. So, truth may sometimes be related to the specific situation or circumstance. But compromise with truth on such pleas must not be frequent and the matter is to be finally decided by the voice of conscience. Gandhi very much believed in the authenticity and efficacy of the voice of conscience, because in the light of the Hindu faith he believed that every individual had a divine element in him in the form of his soul. Therefore, according to Gandhi, the inner voice as conscience would be the sole judge for knowing what is truth or what might be the circumstance in which a compromise with truth might be justified. To the question, 'What is truth?' Gandhi once replied: 'What the voice within tells you'. This shows that for deciding the questions of truth, Gandhi very much depended on the voice of conscience. But this kind of dependence on the authority of conscience has an obvious air of subjectivity about it and there are chances of its being misused by irresponsible or immature persons. Gandhi well visualised the difficulty and therefore he laid down certain strict conditions for those who took the plea of the voice of conscience for taking anything as true or for deciding compromise with truth. He said that before making a compromise with truth on the strength of the call of the conscience, a man must have fully disciplined himself by cultivating the virtues of the truthfulness, purity of heart, selflessness, a*parigrah* etc. In the words of Gandhi, one must have reduced himself to zero, before he begins claiming the realization of truth or the recognition of the real situation in which truth might be compromised for falsehood on the basis of the voice of his conscience. To quote Gandhi's own words in this connection, "If you would swim on the bosom of the ocean of Truth, you must reduce yourself to zero"[2], or again, "The path of truth is as narrow as it is straight.... It is like balancing oneself on the edge of a sword."[3] Thus to tread the path of truth with an honest motive and a strong resolve without self-creating situations of compromise is not a very easy task according to Gandhi. It is as he says, a *tapasyā*, which requires self-suffering and self-renunciation.

We have talked above of the two senses of 'truth' of which the second, i.e., the moral sense, has drawn much attention from Gandhi. But Gandhi has used the word 'Truth' in a third sense also and that is the metaphysical sense. Let us now come to this metaphysical sense of the word 'Truth' in which Gandhi has used it most prominently. we have seen in our analysis of his concept of God that he has identified *Satya* (Truth) with God. Formerly he used to say 'God is Truth' but later on with a mind to lay greater emphasis on Truth and Virtue, he identified it with God and began to say 'Truth is God'. Here he seems to take Truth or *Satya* in the sense of *Sat* which means entire existence or existence as such. He has further identified it with the Law, the *Dharma* or the *Ṛta*. In short, he has identified *Satya* with that basic reality which underlies the entire universe and which holds and sustains it. We find everything of the universe as fleeting and changing but *Satya* is that fundamental basis of the universe which endures amidst all changes. It is clear that in identifying *Satya* with *Sat, Ṛta* or *Dharma* and finally with God, Gandhi has tried to preserve within the concept of *Satya* all the metaphysical and moral overtones of these terms of Hindu tradition. In fact, in the Hindu tradition, *Satya* has always been taken as a synonym of reality, while *Mithyā* has been taken as a synonym of unreality or appearance.

Although *Satya* or Truth in itself is, according to Gandhi, one and absolute, still there is a sense in which there can be a distinction between Absolute and Relative truth. The distinction is based on the plea that although Truth is absolute, it can be realised by human beings only relatively. Human beings suffer from serious limitations of vision and therefore they are not capable of realising truth in all its aspects, in its entire wholeness. Everybody could realise truth in his own partial way only relatively. Here Gandhi so often cited the Indian story of six blind men who wanted to know the truth of an elephant in its entirety by touching it. But what was the result? One who touched the feet of the elephant exclaimed that it was like the trunk of a tree, one who touched the tail of the elephant exclaimed that it was like a rope, one who touched the body exclaimed that it was like a rough surface, and so on. But we can well see that the truth about the elephant realised by each blind man here was only partial and relative. Truth has several aspects but man due to his truncated vision could not see all the aspects of Truth simultaneously. He could view only a few and therefore his vision of truth will necessarily be partial and relative. However, although the truth realised by each man is only partial and relative, it has its value in as much as it is only through such relative and particular instances of truth that the Absolute Truth deciphers itself to us. Gandhi took the relative truth as his 'beacon' which showed him light and worked as his guide. He knew that although it was not the Absolute Truth, it was still a glimpse of Him which should serve as his master and guide. As Gandhi himself said, "The relative truth must, meanwhile, be my bacon, my shield and buckler.... I have gone forward according to my light. Often in my progress I have had faint glimpses of the Absolute Truth, God and daily the conviction is growing upon me that He alone is real and all else is unreal."[4]

But here one thing is very important. The man realising the relative truth must not take his realisation as absolute and exclusive. He should rather also realise that whatever truth he has known is only partial and therefore other's statements about the self-same reality might also be true from their own specific stand point. Here Gandhi seems fully impressed by the Jain doctrines of *anekāntvāda* and *syādvāda*. The former says that reality has innumerable aspects of which anybody can know only a few from a specific standpoint. Therefore nobody should claim exclusive validity for his knowledge of something. And this leads to the second, that is *syadvada*, which roughly says that one should, therefore, utter any judgement about anything by adding *syāda* towards the beginning of his judgment so that his judgment may be taken as beginning with the prefix 'Relatively speaking' for *Syāda* actually means relatively speaking.

We have seen earlier in connection with truth as a moral virtue that for the observance of the moral virtue of truth, fearlessness *(Abhay)*, non-possession *(aparigrah)*etc. are necessary. Only he can speak the truth consistently who is fearless and selfless. But according to Gandhi these two are necessary not only for the worship of truthfulness, but also for the realisation of Truth in its metaphysical sense. About the need of fearlessness in search of Truth, Gandhi has said, "The pursuit of Truth is true *bhakti* (devotion). It is the path that leads to God and therefore there is no place in it for cowardice, no place for defeat. It is the talisman by which death itself becomes the portal of life eternal."[5] Similarly, about the need of non-possessions or selflessness, Gandhi has said, "Possession implies provision for the future. A seeker after Truth.... cannot hold anything against tomorrow. God never stores for tomorrow..... Perfect fulfilment of the ideal of non-possession requires that man should, like the birds, have no roof over his head, no clothing and no stock of food for the morrow. He will indeed need his daily bread, but it will be God's business, and not his, to provide for it."[6] Again, "From the standpoint of pure Truth, the body too is a possession. It has been truly said that desire for enjoyment creates bodies for the soul. When this desire vanishes, there remains no further need for the body...."[7] But because so long as one is alive, it is not possible to be completely non-possessed, that according to Gandhi, perfect realisation of Truth is not possible as long as we have the ephemeral body. As Gandhi has himself said, "It is impossible for us to realise perfect Truth so long as we are imprisoned in this mortal frame. We can only visualise it in our imagination. We cannot, through the instrumentality of this ephemeral body, see face to face Truth which is eternal. That is why in the last resort one must depend on faith."[8]

(B) AHIMSĀ (NON-VIOLENCE)

As we have said earlier, Gandhi is more known to the world for his concept and practice of *ahimsā* than for anything else. Of course, the concept of *ahimsā* has not originated with Gandhi. He has rather adopted it from the long traditions of Hinduism, Buddhism and Jainism in which the concept played a very vital role. In these traditions *ahimsā* was regarded as the highest *dharm* and was taken as an essential means to liberation. It formed a vital part of the spiritual discipline taught by the *Yoga* of Patanjali. However, in the Jain and Buddha traditions as well as in the Hindu epics, complete *ahimsā* could be successfully practised only buy a saint or a monk. But Gandhi refused to accept different standards for saints and ordinary people. He was a practical idealist, who believed that all the higher moral and spiritual virtues could be practiced by ordinary people and saints alike, if the former also made sincere efforts for them. According to him, *ahimsā* was the law of human species. *Himsā* was meant for the brutes alone. Thus non-violence was not meant for the monks and saints alone. It was meant for the common man as well. As he declared quite unambiguously, "I am not a visionary. I claim to be a practical idealist. The religion of non-violence is not meant merely for the *rishis* and saints. It is meant for the common people as well. Non-violence is the law of our species as violence is the law of the brute."[9] Thus by taking *ahimsā* as engrained in the very nature of man, Gandhi inflicted a special responsibility upon man to observe ahimsā in all sorts of activities in life. Moreover by practicing *ahimsā* in letter and spirit throughout his life Gandhi became more or less identified with *ahimsā* and Gandhi and *ahimsā* became almost synonymous terms.

1. Meaning of *Ahimsā*

Let us now try to see what *ahimsā* actually meant for Gandhi. The word *ahimsā* literally means non-injury, or more narrowly, non-killing. But taken in somewhat a wider connotation, it means abstaining from harming anyone in any form. It implies complete renunciation of will or intention to hurt or harm anybody in any way. It is abstention from hostile thought, word or deed towards anybody. Gandhi used the word in this wider connotation. In fact he used it in its widest possible connotation and distinguished between its negative and positive senses in the following words, "In its negative form it means not injuring any living being, whether by body or by mind. I may not, therefore, hurt the person or any wrong-doer or bear any ill will to him and so cause him mental suffering. This statement does not cover suffering caused to the wrong-doer by natural acts of mine which do not proceed from an ill will.... *Ahimsā* requires deliberate self-suffering, not a deliberate injuring of the supposed wrong-doer..... In its positive form *Ahimsā* means the largest love, the greatest charity. If I am a follower of *ahimsā*, I must love my enemy. I must apply the same rules to the wrong-doer, who is my enemy or a stranger to me, as I would to my wrong-doing father or son."[10]

The quotation clearly shows that Gandhi used the term *ahimsā* in two senses-one negative and the other positive. In its negative sense *ahimsā* meant for him non-injury in all its forms–vocal, mental and active physical. But *ahimsā*, for him, was not only this. It had a positive side also and in its positive side or sense it meant love and charity. Then again, this love or charity was not meant only for one's own men or for some stray wrong doer, but also for one's enemy. The real test of one's *ahimsā* was, according to Gandhi, that the man possessed no ill will even towards his enemy. He rather loved him as he would love his wrong doing father or son. Furthermore, true observance of *ahimsā* required self-suffering rather than inflicting suffering upon the wrong doer. Thus it is clear that to be a follower of *ahimsā* in the Gandhian sense is not a very easy task. It is, as Gandhi sometimes himself said, like a *tapasyā*. According to Gandhi, a follower of true *ahimsā* must always be ready to die without any desire even to hurt or kill anyone. And obviously, this is not an easy task. Gandhi distinguished between three kinds of *himsā* and took abstention from all of them as *ahimsā*. There is, first of all *krta himsā*, i.e., violence done by one's own self. Then there is *kārita himsā*, i.e., violence instigated and got done by someone else. Lastly, there is *anumodit himsā*, i.e., *himsā* being done, of course, by someone else without my consent or advise, but I, instead of preventing the person from doing *himsā*, am giving my indirect support by watching passively the *himsā* being done before my eyes. Simply looking on to an act of himself without making any active effort to prevent it is also *himsā*, according to Gandhi. I am in a way approving the *himsā* being committed by someone else. This act of indirect approval of an act of *himsā* is as good *himsā* as done by one's own self according to Gandhi. All the three kinds of act are equally *himsā* according to Gandhi and therefore any follower of *ahimsā* must abstain from all of these. This also shows the fairly wide sense in which Gandhi took the term *ahimsā*. Professor Raghavan Iyer has tried to incorporate the full sense of the wide connotation given to the word *ahimsā* by Gandhi in the following words, "The yoga of ahimsā consists in the devising of means and doing of acts, calculated to check the evil tendency of *himsā* and to eliminate to the best of one's power the effects of the commission of such acts from human society."[11]

Sometimes, Gandhi used the term *'ahimsā'* in such a wide sense that he virtually included almost all the moral virtues like humility, forgiveness, love, charity, selflessness, fearlessness, strength, non-attachment, meekness, innocence etc. within it.

The principle of *ahimsā*, he sometimes said, is hurt by every evil thought, by undue haste, by lying, by hatred, by wishing ill to anybody, and so on. Similarly, he stretched the meaning of the word *'himsā'* to include "trickery, falsehood, intrigue, chicanery and deceitfulness." In short, "all unfair and foul means come under the category of *himsā*", according to him. This is all in a sense confusing and indicative of somewhat a loose use of terms by the non-technical philosopher Gandhi. But if we remember that Gandhi was not a theoretical analyst of terms, rather he was a practical philosopher, we can find ample sense in his using the terms *'himsā'* and *'ahimsā'* in such a broad perspective.

Some of the moral virtues included under the meanings of the word *'ahimsā'* express the direct meanings of the term and some extend supporting hands without which the virtue of *ahimsā* or positive love and charity could not be practised. For example, unless one is selfless and non-attached, one cannot be truly able to follow the path of love and charity. Similarly, arrogance, hard-headedness and cruelty cannot accommodate *ahimsā*. For that, virtues like humanity, meekness etc. are necessary. So, to be truly non-violent in the Gandhian sense, it is really necessary to follow all the moral virtues pointed out by him as carrying the sense of *ahimsā*. Gandhi seems here as holding on to the Buddhist and Jain views that all sins are in a sense modifications of the one basic sin of *himsā* and therefore if one wanted to be a follower of *ahimsā*, he must give up all such vices as falsehood, deceitfulness, etc.

Gandhi, of course, took *ahimsā* in its positive sense as love, but he preferred the word charity to love. For, according to him, the former implied pity for the wrong-doer. He said, "*Ahimsā* is love in the Paulion sense, and yet something more than the 'Love' defined by St. Paul, although I know St. Paul's beautiful definition is good enough for all practical purposes."[12] Although Gandhi used the word '*ahimsā*' with the positive force of love and charity, he preferred using the negative term non-violence for it because in his view this term included many more virtues within it besides love and charity. We have seen that Gandhi sometimes included almost all the important moral virtues within *ahimsā*. *Ahimsā* for him was not only a desirable moral virtue, but also the most fundamental and perhaps the only way in which one could express his respect and regard for the innate worth and value of all human beings, and for that matter, of all beings. Because all beings are the expressions of the same basic Truth, *ahimsā* must be our fundamental law. It is an essential and universal obligation without which we would cease to be human. The creed of *ahimsā* presupposes the existence of an immortal essence in the human personality. It is the recognition of this essence which gives man the courage of readiness to die without any intention to kill, which is the essence of *ahimsā* according to Gandhi. *Ahimsā* is soul-force, said Gandhi. Without this soul-force, nobody can be truly non-violent. Non-violence is possible only by the strength of the soul. We have seen that a follower of *ahimsā* must suffer himself instead of inflicting suffering upon the opponent, and this involves tremendous inner strength on one's part. A man of weak determination can never be able to do so. This is why Gandhi has taken *ahimsā* as a weapon of the strong, and not of the weak and the coward. Cowardice and *ahimsā* are contradictory terms according to him, because whereas the latter emanates from true inner strength of the soul, the former emanates from weakness." Non-violence and cowardice go ill together", said Gandhi. He further said, "Non-violence presupposes ability to strike. It is a conscious, deliberate restraint put upon one's desire for vengeance."[13] One who is non-violent due to lack of strength is not really non-violent. One is really non-violent when one has the ability to strike, but does not strike due to the deliberate restraint he has put upon himself out of inner love and charity even for the enemy. So true non-violence resides in the mind. It is an inner disposition. If we keep ill will and hatred from within but do not outwardly strike, that is a sign of cowardice and weakness, not of genuine non-violence. As Gandhi said, "Non-violence to be potent force must begin with the mind. Non-violence of the mere body without the co-operation of the mind is non-violence of the weak and cowardly, and has therefore no potency."[14] A coward could never be non-violent according to Gandhi. There was hope for a violent man to be some day non-violent, because by proper training and education he could be reformed, but a coward could never be non-violent, because there was a conceptual contradiction between cowardice and non-violence. As Gandhi said, "My creed of non-violence is an extremely active force. It has no room for cowardice or even weakness. There is hope for a violent man to be some day non-violent, but there is none for a coward."[15] Gandhi preferred violence to cowardice. That is, he preferred a man who could resort to violence on occasions of duties such as defending the honour of women or of one's nation to him who was a silent spectator to tyranny, oppression, dishonouring of women etc. due to cowardice. He openly said, "I do believe that, where there is only a choice between cowardice and violence, I would advise violence. I would rather have India resort to arms in order to defend her honour than that she should, in a cowardly manner, become or remain a helpless witness to her own dishonour."[16] Or again, he was so clear as to assert the following, "I have therefore said more than once in these pages that if we do not know how to defend ourselves, our women and our places of worship by the force of suffering, i.e., non-violence, we must, if we are men, be at least able to defend all these by fighting."[17]However, there is no doubt about it that Gandhi preferred non-violence supremely to violence, but the non-violence he preferred was that of the able and the strong who were non-violent by the strength of their soul-force, and not the pretended non-violence of the weak and the coward.

We have said above that according to Gandhi *ahimsā* is the law of the human species and therefore it is to be followed by the saints and the common people alike. But true *ahimsā* in its honest spirit is not something very easy to follow and practise. Even outward *himsā*, which is *himsā* in the most obvious form, cannot be fully avoided so long as we are alive. Gandhi himself recognised this fact when he said, "We are helpless mortals caught in the conflagration of *himsā*. Man cannot live for a moment without causing or unconsciously committing outward *himsā*."[18]Again, he said, "*Ahimsā* is a quality of the disembodied soul alone."[19] So long as one is bound in the shackles of flesh, he cannot avoid *himsā* completely in all its forms. Bodily existence itself involves some amount of *himsā* for survival. No matter howsoever careful and compassionate one may be, he cannot escape committing some violence. Gandhi recognized this fact when he said, "It is impossible to sustain one's body without the destruction of other bodies to some extent."[20] Similarly, as social beings also we sometimes have to resort to *himsā* and such *himsā* Gandhi did not prohibit in an unqualified manner. He did not want to make a fetish of *ahimsā* and in the spirit of the Gita he took the observance of one's *dharma* (Svadharma) as one's supreme duty. In cases of moral dilemma when circumstances required *himsā* and there was no way out for fulfilling one's moral duty without resorting to *himsā*, Gandhi allowed it. Gandhi has cited the example of a man who in a fit of madness goes about with a sword swaying in his hand and killing people indiscriminately. No body dares capturing this demon alive. Now, what to do in such a situation? It is necessary to kill such a man for avoiding further *himsā* and for protecting other members of the society. Similarly, there might be other situations in which killing would be necessary as a moral duty.

But here a problem arises. If *himsā* is allowed sometimes on consideration of unavoidable moral duty, then anybody can resort to *himsā* on that plea and *ahimsā* would no longer remain a universal moral principle. What would Gandhi have to say as an answer to this problem? Gandhi's intention of making *ahimsā* as absolute moral principle posed real problems for him, but he tried to solve them in the true spirit of being a practical idealist. If we pick up some thread from the several statements made by him that we have quoted earlier, we may find a few points which would explain why in a sense Gandhi took his principle of *ahimsā* as absolute but still allowed certain exceptions which would not jeopardise his basic position on *ahimsā*. First of all, mere outward non-killing is not *ahimsā* according to him. Real *ahimsā* lies in our heart, in our intention and will. So, even if one overtly kills, but behind that killing he has no ill will, no selfish intention, and his action is being guided by a pure, non-attached sense of duty, his killing is not *himsā*. Gandhi distinguished between *himsā* and *ahimsā* by indicating that *himsā* meant killing from a sense of ill will or a motive of selfishness, anger etc. and *ahimsā* meant refraining from so doing. As Gandhi said, "Ahimsā does not simply mean non-killing. Himsā means causing pain to or killing any one out of anger, or from a selfish purpose or with the intention of injuring it. Refraining from so doing is ahimsā."[21] At least in its negative sense *ahimsā* certainly means this. This is also clear from a part of the statement of Gandhi which we have quoted on our preceding pages of this chapter by way of depicting his negative and positive senses of the term '*ahimsā*'- "This statement does not cover suffering caused to the wrong-doer by natural acts of mine which do not proceed from ill will......" Thus, it is not very easy to justify any action of *himsā* on the plea that it was a part of one's moral obligation or *svadharma*. The conditions are very stringent. It is not a very easy task to act in the true spirit of the *Bhagavad Gītā*, i.e., in a perfectly detached manner. Only that overt *himsā* may be justified which is done in a detached manner as a part of one's moral duty and not any kind of killing. A soldier, so long as he has chosen to do his duty as a soldier, must fight, but the moment he opts for *ahimsā*, he must give up his job as a soldier. Thus, Gandhi's principle of *ahimsā* is not absolute in the sense that it admits of no exceptions. It is absolute in the sense that carried out in the true sense of non-attachment, love and charity towards all beings, it informs the spirit within about the circumstances in which violence becomes necessary. In such situations, the soul knows that it is doing something wrong because it is unavoidable and is filled with a sense of remorse and distress. Perfect nonviolence is not possible in human body. A man, therefore, is to do what it is morally possible for him to do in the particular circumstances. As Gandhi said in this connection, "Perfect non-violence whilst you are inhabiting the body is only a theory like Euclid's point or straight line, but we have to endeavour every moment of our lives."[22] All these considerations show how Gandhi conceived of *ahimsā* as a great moral virtue, rather the greatest moral virtue, which included within it almost all the high ethical virtues, but at the same time he realized the practical difficulties of the ordinary people in observing the vow in true letter and spirit without any exception. He was a practical idealist and not utopian and therefore he only talked of such virtues and now which could be practically observed. Still he did never make those spiritual and moral virtues very cheap on the ground of practical difficulties. His own life is a true example of the observance of the virtue of *himsā* through the various complicated phases of life. 'Life', Gandhi rightly held, "is not a single straight line, it is a bundle of duties very often conflicting. And one is called upon continually to make one's choice between one duty and another."[23] But despite the zigzag ways of life, Gandhi stood firm to his faith in *ahimsā* in more or less an absolute manner and in that lies his greatness.

But again a question may face us: if mere non killing is not a *himsā* and killing sometimes may be a necessary duty, as in case of the lunatic referred earlier, then why not kill all those who oppress mankind? Gandhi perhaps would have never allowed it because he was of the firm opinion that no human being is so bad as to be beyond redemption. No human being is so perfect as to warrant him destroying him whom he wrongly considers to be wholly evil."[24] We have seen that Gandhi believed in the inherent goodness of man and according to him no man was such who could not be reformed by proper education. What was required for this kind of reformation was unqualified love for the man with a readiness for self-suffering. Here it may be asked: then why did Gandhi recommend killing of the lunatic who went about killing people with the sword in his hand? Why could he be not reformed? But here we must mark that the imaginary lunatic of Gandhi's conception was such whom 'no one dares to capture alive'. If he could also be captured alive then Gandhi would never have recommended his killing. He was of the firm faith that "there was no one so fallen in this world but could be converted by love."[25]

2. Ahimsā and Satya

Ahimsā has very intimate relationship with truth according to Gandhi. In fact truth is the goal and *ahimsā* is its surest means. On the face, it seems that truth is somewhat superior to *ahimsā* because the former is the goal and the latter only a means. But really it is not so. Means and end are unextricating bound up with each other according to Gandhi. The two are mutually convertible terms. Gandhi was of firm faith that a good end could be achieved only by a good means. An end, howsoever good it might be, could not be desirable unless it was attained through a good means. Here Gandhi was exactly echoing the following words of A. Huxley, "... the means employed inevitably determine the nature of the results achieved, whereas, however good the end aimed maybe, it's goodness is powerless to counter fact the effects of bad means we used to reach it."[26] For Gandhi it was the means, and not the end, which was to be taken more care of because if the means was good, the end was bound to be good but not conversely. So, *ahimsā*, even if it was only a means, was as a matter of fact everything. As Gandhi remarked, "I would say 'means are after all everything'. As the means so the end.... There is no wall of separation between means and end.... Realization of the goal is in exact proportion to that of means."[27] So truth and *ahimsā* are very intimately related and it is difficult to separate them. As Gandhi himself would say, "*Ahimsā* and truth are so interwind that it is practically impossible to disentangle and seperate them. They are like the two sides of a coin, or rather of a smooth unstamped metallic disc. Who can say which is the obverse, and which the reverse?"[28]To practice *ahimsā*, according to Gandhi, would be to realise truth and so realised truth would be to practice *ahimsā*. Nothing would be better than to quote his own words in this connection, *"Ahimsā* is my God and Truth is my God. When I look to *Ahimsā*, Truth says 'Find it through me'. When I look to Truth, *Ahimsā* says 'Find it through me'."[29] The words amply shows that according to Gandhi Truth and *Ahimsā* are to be realised through each other. Both are inextricably bound up. The intimate relationship between Truth and *ahimsā,* that Gandhi wanted to convey through his above cited statements, is historically rooted in the Hindu, Buddhist and the Jain traditions. It also follows from Gandhi's own metaphysical beliefs regarding the nature of God and man. We know that the word *'Rta'* as used in the Vedas refers to the principle of moral order inherent in the universe as well as to the overall cosmic equilibrium. Later on this word seems to be replaced by the word *'Dharma,* which means that which sustains or upholds. In this sense the word refers to the Moral Law which maintains the whole world, including the individual and the human society. This cosmic law has been identified with Truth in the Vedas as well as in the later Hindu tradition.

The *Brihadāranayaka Upnishada* says that with the help of *Staya,* which is *Dharma,* even the weakest could gain victory over the strongest. It is also said simultaneously that whatever is attended by non-violence *(ahimsā)* is the *Dharma,* and one could attain to Truth through non-violence. Non-violence is the highest dharma *(Ahimsā paramo dharmah).* Bhisma in the *Mahābhārata* declared that abstention from injury to creatures was the real *dharma.* Hence *Satya* and *ahimsā* have been traditionally identified with *Dharma* in Hinduism. In the Buddhist tradition, *himsā* and *asatya* alike form the sin of separateness *(attavāda).* It is due to this that man is engaged in narrow self-interest and resorts to violence and untruth. Similarly in the Jain texts it is said that *asat* inevitably leads to violence *(himsā).* The individual, when becomes free from the passion of egoism and *himsā,* is capable of mirroring the highest truth or reality from within him.

Again, the intimate relationship between *Satya* and *ahimsā* follows from Gandhi's own beliefs regarding the nature of God and man also. Gandhi believed that there was an essential unity between God and human self and also between one self and another. As a matter of fact, he believed in the essential unity of all beings, because God or Truth was present in all of them. As he said, "I believe in Advaita, I believe in the essential unity of man and, for that matter, of all that lives."[30] And when there is no essential difference between one self and another, violence or injury to any other becomes injury to one's own self. Thus, the non-dualist position of Gandhi actually implies the intimate relationship between Truth and *ahimsā*. Again, we have seen that non-possession and absolute lack of self-interest are essential conditions according to Gandhi both for the realization of Truth and for the practice of *ahimsā*. So long as one is attached to worldly things and works for one's own selfish interest, one can neither practise truthfulness and *ahimsā,* nor can he be able to realize Truth. Thus, it may be seen how intimately Truth and *ahimsā* are related together according to Gandhi.

In formulating his concept of *ahimsā* and in making it the main moral and spiritual weapon of his life-journey, Gandhi was definitely influenced from the various sides, but still in an important sense his concept of *ahimsā* was uniquely his own. The lesson of *ahimsā* is present in every religion and Gandhi was well aware of it. He repeatedly pointed out that *ahimsā* was advocated in the *Gita*, the *Bible*, the *Koran* and much more particularly in the teachings of Buddhism and Jainism. But again, he himself claimed, that his conception of *ahimsā* was in many respects independent of the sanction of the scriptures. However, the impact of none of these religious texts and traditions on Gandhi can be underrated. As a young man Gandhi became familiar with the principle of winning over an enemy by love by the poems of the Gujarati poet, Samal Bhatta. But when he read the *Gitā*, he based his concept of *ahimsā* on it by linking it to the ideas of non-attachment, freedom from hatred, anger, pride etc. The teachings of the *New Testament* on love had a very definite and great effect on Gandhi's concept of *ahimsā* in its positive form. Gandhi himself recognised this impact when he referred to the event of the crucification of Jesus in the following words, "He who when being killed bears no anger against his murderer and even asks God to forgive him is truly non-violent.

History relates this of Jesus Christ. With his dying breath on his cross, he is reported to have said: 'Father, forgive them for they know not what they do'."[31] Gandhi found a tremendous support for his principle of *ahimsā* in the following lines of the *New Testament* "You have heard that it hath been said: Thou shalt love thy neighbour and hate thy enemy. But I say to you: Love your enemies: do good to them that hate you and pray for them that persecute and calumniate you...... For if you love them that love you, what reward shall you have? Do not even the publicans do this? And if you salute your brethren only, what do you more? Do not also the heathens do this?" These lines of the *New Testament* had an obvious echo in Gandhi's concept of *ahimsā* when he said that *ahimsā* meant loving even those who hated you and not simply those who loved you. Gandhi spoke of loving enemies in the same way in which we love our wrong doing father and son. Gandhi wholeheartedly shared the view of the Buddha on war: "Victory breeds hatred, because the conquered is unhappy". Similarly, he very much shared the sermon of the Buddha: "Let a man conquer anger by love, evil by good, greed by liberality and lie by truth". He also believed like the Buddha that society was held together only by non-violence. Albert Schweitzer seems to hold that Gandhi was definitely influenced by the Buddha in his concept of *ahimsā*, but then he in some sense went even beyond Buddha. Schweitzer remarks: "Gandhi continues what the Buddha began. In the Buddha the spirit of love set itself the task of creating different spiritual conditions in the world; in Gandhi it undertakes to transform *all* worldly conditions."[32] Thus the Buddha exerted definite influence on Gandhi in the formation of his concepts of *ahimsā* and *Satyāgraha*. Gandhi was also impressed in this respect, as we have pointed out earlier also, by the long and peaceful suffering of Ali, the son-in-law of Prophet Muhammad. In his suffering he saw a glaring example of non-violence and *satyāgraha*. Jainism had perhaps the greatest effect on Gandhi in this respect, because, as we know, he through his father remained very much in close contact with the Jains. It is an open fact that *ahimsā* is regarded as the greatest and the most essential virtue according to Jainism both for the common man and the monk. However, Gandhi did not like the extreme form in which *ahimsā* is tried to be observed in Jainism. As a practical idealist, we have seen, he realised the limitations of ordinary men and honestly recognised that it was not possible for ordinary people to be perfect followers of *ahimsā* so long as they were embodied.

Besides the various religions which had their impact on Gandhi in the formation of his concept of ahimsā, what made a crucial impact on him in this regard was Tolstoy's *The Kingdom of God is within you*. Gandhi himself acknowledged his indebtedness to Tolstoy in this respect when he gratefully declared, "For inculating this true and higher type of *Ahimsā* (i.e., the *ahimsā* of positive love) amongst us, Tolstoy's life with its ocean-like love should serve as a beacon light and a never-failing source of inspiration....."[33] Tolstoy appealed to Gandhi most as an apostle of non-violence in its positive sense of love.

(C) SATYĀGRAHA

We have seen how according to Gandhi Truth and non-violence are very intimately connected. The concept of *Satyāgraha* is a concrete or practical expression of the intimate relationship between the two. For Gandhi, Truth was the end and *ahimsā* the means. *Satyāgraha* is the relentless search after Truth through the means of ahimsā. The concept of *Satyāgraha*, therefore, represents a real synthesis between the twin concepts of *satya* and *ahimsā*. It is a symbol of the practical application of the two concepts in real life. As a matter of fact, through the concept of *Satyāgraha* and the practice thereof throughout his life in all its spheres, Gandhi gave a real shape to his essential metaphysical and ethical beliefs.

The word '*Satyāgraha*' literally means *āgraha* for '*Satya*'. The word '*āgraha*' comes from the root '*grah*' which means 'to get hold of', 'to hold fast to', 'to seize upon'. *Āgraha* for *Satya*, therefore, means holding on to or holding fast to or seizing upon Truth. It may also be taken to mean, by extension, searching for Truth relentlessly, fearlessly and tenaciously. Now, this *āgraha* for Truth must be non-violent according to Gandhi. In no case it should be violent. As a matter of fact, Satyāgraha was practised in India as well as abroad even before the name was given to it. Wherever and whenever there is an example of holding fast to truth in face of even the most cruel oppression without any attempt to resist the oppression through a violent means and by bearing endless suffering upon one's own self, that is an example of *Satyāgraha*. Such examples of *Satyāgraha* may be found in the sufferings of Harischandra and Prahlād in ancient India. In the West Socrates and Jesus Christ represent the purest form of *Satyāgraha*. The stories of Prahlād and Harischandra found in the ancient Hindu religious tradition had a lifelong influence upon Gandhi. He was really very much impressed by their exemplary devotion to truth combined with the spirit of non-retaliation and self-suffering. Therein lies really the essence of Satyāgraha. Gandhi took Jesus Christ as the 'apostle' of *satyāgraha*. His ungrudging suffering on the Cross combined with the words of love and sympathy for even those who were responsible for his crucifixion is the most glaring example of Satyāgraha. When as a young man Gandhi read the New Testament and specially the Sermon on the Mount, he was simply overjoyed, because he found therein a continuation of his own ideas about *Satya* and *ahimsā (Satyāgraha)*. The concept of *Satyāgraha* was formed under influences from many sides, e. g., from the *Bhagavad-Gītā*, the Sermon on the Mount, the sufferings of Ali (the son-in-law of Prophet Mohammad), and from the writings of Tolstoy & Thoreau. But still there was an originality, a freshness about Gandhi's concept of *Satyāgraha* and his greatest merit lay in his widest possible application of the concept in spheres of individual, social and political life.

Before Gandhi termed his non-violent movement of resisting evil by good as *Satyāgraha,* he called it by the names of passive resistance and *'sadāgraha'*. First of all, on parity of a movement started by the Suffragettes in England, Gandhi termed his movement against the Government of South Africa as passive resistance. Perhaps the only idea that worked at that time in his mind behind calling the movement of his conception as passive resistance was to distinguish it from a movement which was violent and aggressive and which involved active fighting with arms. Because he had planned to resist the evil Government of South Africa in a non-violent manner, he called his method of resistance passive resistance. But he realized it very soon that the name was not adequate to the spirit of his movement. Although it was not active in the sense of armed fighting, still it was not passive. Characterizing the movement as passive implied that it was a movement of the weak. Gandhi, we have seen, took his *ahimsā* as a weapon of the strong, and therefore, he did not like calling his non-violent resistance, passive resistance. Moreover, he wanted to distinguish his movement from that of the Suffragettes, because the latter were not non-violent in principle and their movement had always a scope to be violent and aggressive. The movement of Gandhi's conception was to be in no case aggressive and violent. It was to be based not on any feeling of hatred towards the opponent, rather it had every scope for love and sympathy towards him. Furthermore, Gandhi wanted his movement to be given a characteristically Indian name. With all these ends in view, Gandhi wanted a new name for his non-violent action. One of his fellowmen in South Africa suggested to him the term '*sadāgraha*' which literally means 'firmness in a good cause or in the cause of truth. Gandhi liked the term, but it did not satisfy him fully. He felt that even this term did not give expression to his idea of the new movement fully adequately. He therefore substituted it by the term '*Satyāgraha*', which he felt made his concept of the non-violent movement more explicit and clearer and was linked more closely with his basic concepts of *Satya* and *ahimsā*. As Gandhi himself said in this connection by way of explaining his preference for the term '*Satyāgraha*' to '*sadāgraha*', "I liked the word, but it did not fully represent the whole idea I wished it to connote: I therefore corrected it to '*Satyāgraha*'. Truth (*Satya*) implies love, and firmness *(āgraha)*, and therefore serves as a synonym for force. I thus began to call the Indian movement '*Satyāgraha*', that is to say, the Force which is both of Truth and Love or Non-violence..."[34] Thus, the *Satyāgraha* of Gandhi's conception came to mean Truth-force, Love-force or Soul-force. It proved to be a force generated out of love to conquer or realize Truth. It was not a physical force, but the force of the soul.

Gandhi later on distinguished sharply between passive resistance and *Satyāgraha* and took all those Westerners as ignorant who took Jesus Christ as a passive resister. According to Gandhi, Christ was a champion of *Satyāgraha,* and not of passive resistance. As he said, "Europe mistook the bold and brave resistance of Jesus of Nazareth for passive resistance as if it were of the weak. As I read the New Testament for the first time, I detected no passivity, no weakness about Jesus as depicted in the four gospels and the meaning became clear to me when I read Tolstoy's Harmony of the gospele and his other kindered writings. Has not the West paid too heavily in regarding Jesus as a Passive Resister."[35] Gandhi distinguished between passive resistance and *Satyāgraha* mainly on the following points :

1. *Satyāgraha* is a weapon of the strong, while passive resistance is adopted by the weak.
2. There is no scope for love in passive resistance, but in *Satyāgraha* there is not only no place for hatred, but love for others including the opponent is its essence.
3. The use of physical force is totally forbidden in Satyāgraha, while it is not so in passive resistance.
4. In passive resistance there is always an idea of harassing the other party, but in *Satyāgraha* there is not the remotest idea of harassing or teasing or injuring the opponent in any way.

The concept of *Satyāgraha* involves various elements in it, but some of its essential elements are: non-violence, love, self-suffering and persuasion. Non-violence is really the cornerstone of *Satyāgraha.* It excludes the use of violence in any shape or form, whether in thought, speech or action. According to Gandhi, *Satyāgraha* "is to violence... what light is to darkness."[36] And therefore, in no case a *Satyāgrahi* is to resort to violence. He is to conquer "evil by good, anger by love, untruth by truth, *himsā* by *ahimsā*" A *satyāgrahi*, therefore, must be a true disciple of Lord Buddha and Jesus Christ. We have seen that the non-violence of Gandhi's conception includes all the finer virtues of heart within it, specially the virtues of love and self-suffering. *Satyāgraha* is a relentless pursuit after Truth. It is a non-violent fighting for a just cause. Search after truth or fighting for a just cause may need resisting the most cruel and inhuman behaviour and action of the opponent. But even in resisting the most inhuman of opponents, a

Satyāgrahi is never to resort to hatred or anger. His aim must be to win over the opponent by the power of love. As we know, Gandhi believed in the essential inner goodness and divinity of man, and therefore he had the firm faith that there was no man on earth, howsoever cruel or inhuman outwardly, who could not be won over by the force of true love. He advised every *satyāgrahi* to work with this firm faith in the inner goodness of man. As he said, "It is an article of faith with every *satyāgrahi* that there is no one so fallen in this world but can be converted by love?"[37] The aim of *Satyāgraha* is conversion, not coercion. The heart of the opponent is to be won over by love and persuasion and he is really to be converted. That is the true art of *Satyāgraha*.

Such an art of conversion may require patient self-suffering. For that, a *Satyāgrahi* has to be always prepared. Gandhi always said that *Satyāgraha* was a *tapasyā*, a *dharma-yuddha*. And for that self-suffering and self-sacrifice, in the spirit of the *Gītā*, were essentially required. Gandhi has really very much emphasized the role of self-suffering in *Satyāgraha*. This self-suffering requires the inner force of one's soul. Hence it is that *Satyāgraha* has always been taken as the soul-force. When the *Satyāgrahi* inflicts voluntary self-suffering for the cause of Truth, his soul-force generates a potency which affects the opponent. There is a bond of spiritual unity between one man and another according to Gandhi and therefore the potency generated by the genuine self-suffering of a man upsets the moral balance of the opponent and he has to realize the mistake of his approach. Suffering, said Gandhi, "will melt the stoniest heart of the stoniest fanatic."[38] Gandhi realized that even if men are rational by nature, they do not come to understand the nature of Truth due to long cherished prejudices. The appeal of reason therefore does not always work. In such cases, it is the self-suffering which is the most effective weapon for arousing good sense and justice from within a man. It touches the heart of the opponent and opens his inner eyes of understanding. As Gandhi said, "I have come to this fundamental conclusion that if you want something really important to be done, you must not merely satisfy the reason, you must move the heart also. The appeal of reason is more to the head, but the penetration of the heart comes from suffering. It opens up the inner understanding of man. Suffering is the badge of the human race, not the sword."[39] In case suffering fails to make a direct appeal to the soul of the oppressor, it would arouse public opinion, which the oppressor would have to honour at last. If the suffering fails to do even that, it would at least purify the sufferer. Suffering is therefore a means of self-purification. It "brings its own joy which surpasses all other joys." Moreover, in accordance with his belief in the law of *Karma*, Gandhi believed that one's suffering in the present life for the cause of Truth would result in future gain. So self-suffering in the true spirit of love devoid of anger and hatred never failed to produce results. It was really the kernel of *Satyāgraha*.

The concept of *Satyāgraha* as outlined above was put to practice by Gandhi in various forms, of which the following three are very important—civil disobedience, non-cooperation and fasting. However, *Satyāgraha* is to be identified with neither of these three. *Satyāgraha*, as Gandhi said, is a big tree of which these are only branches. *Satyāgraha* is a much broader concept than any of these. Civil disobedience is nothing but the disobedience or breach of the unjust and immoral laws of the State with civility. In Gandhi's words, it is "civil breach of unmoral statutory enactments.[40] The expression 'civil disobedience', as Gandhi himself accepted, was first coined by Thoreau to signify his own resistance to the law of the State. But civil disobedience of Thoreau's conception was not necessarily to be of a non-violent nature, because as Gandhi himself said, "Thoreau was not perhaps an out and out champion of non-violence."[41] But the civil disobedience of Gandhi's conception must necessarily be non-violent. In due course, Gandhi substituted 'civil resistance' for 'civil disobedience', because he thought that the former conveyed the non-violent character of his movement better. Non-cooperation, according to Gandhi, chiefly implies the withdrawal of co-operation from a state which, in the non-cooperator's view, has become corrupt. It is in Gandhi's words 'an expression of anguished love'. As non-cooperation also is a branch of *Satyāgraha*, this also must be non-violent in character. Again, because both of these are, in a sense, a kind of non-violent fight against an unjust State, both of them imply suffering in the form of imprisonment or such other torture from the side of the State. Suffering, we have seen, is the essence of *Satyāgraha* and therefore a follower of civil disobedience or non-cooperation should be ready for suffering by courting arrest or by bearing other tortures. In no case, however, he is to retort or retaliate in a violent manner. In directing both civil disobedience and non-cooperation against the State, Gandhi felt that the citizen was entitled to appeal to *dharma*, with which both *Satya* and *ahimsā* were identified. Gandhi was of opinion that "Disobedience to the law of the State becomes a pre-emptory duty when it comes in conflict with the law of God."[42] Thus according to Gandhi, civil disobedience and non-co-operation were both non-violent methods of resolving conflicts as well as peaceful devices for producing positive changes in social and political life. In either case, however, Gandhi seemed more concerned with affecting prevalent attitudes and values than with obstructing particular policies.

The most potent and effective weapon of a *satyāgrahi* is fasting. Civil disobedience and non-cooperation imply suffering inflicted by the opponent, but fasting implies self-inflicted suffering. It is thus the purest form of *Satyāgraha*. It is the highest means of self-purification. It is to be used as a penance or as a means of demonstrating spirit's supremacy over the flesh. In Hinduism fasting has been taken as a penance and in Jainism and Islam, it has been an effective religious vow for self-purification. Gandhi was really touched by all these effects of fasting as mentioned in these religions. However, as a weapon of the *satyāgrahi*, fasting has got a very limited application and is to be resorted to on rare occasions. Furthermore, it is to be resorted to by only those who are strictly disciplined and who have got spiritual fitness and clear vision. Faith in God is also necessary, for without that the necessary inner strength for suffering cannot be had. Moreover, in a *Satyāgrahi's* fast, there can be no room for anger, impatience and selfishness. A fast undertaken for selfish ends is not the fast of a *satyāgrahi*.

It is rather a *durāgrahi's* fast or hunger-strike, which Gandhi condemned like anything. When taken with unselfish motives, it has the tremendous force of converting or reforming the wrong-doer. Gandhi acknowledged the worth of fasting in the following words, "My repeated experience...... has been that when applied it has been the most infallible remedy...."[43] It is, according to Gandhi, the surest means of mass-conversion. "The Only language they (the masses) understand is the language of the heart: and fasting when utterly unselfish, is the language of the heart."[44] Gandhi so often resorted to fasting for disengaging Hindus and Muslims from rioting and this had tremendous effect. One important condition that Gandhi added to the use of fasting as a *satyāgrahi's* weapon was that no fast should be taken against an opponent; it was to be taken only against one's near and dear with a view to reform him of them from wrong-doing. As Gandhi clearly said, "fasting can be resorted to only against a lover, not to extort rights, but to reform him, as when a son fasts for a father who drinks...... fasted to reform those who loved me."[45] If fasting is directed against an opponent, it becomes a form of coercion and ceases to be non-violent.

However, as exceptions to the above general principle that fasting should not be taken against an opponent, Gandhi himself fasted at least thrice against the British Government. But if the circumstances under which Gandhi resorted to fasting against the Government are analysed, we can see that they were instances of such wrong-doings on the part of the government that the anguished soul of Gandhi could find no way out to resist them non-violently except by resorting to this last *satyāgrahi* remedy. Gandhi was consistent here in being faithful to his principle that fasting was to be resorted to as the last non-violent remedy, when all other non-violent means were exhausted. Fasting in these cases was, of course, in a sense coercion, because it was like taking advantage of the weak and vulnerable aspect of the opponent, but Gandhi's justification for these instances of fasting may be seen in his following words taken from a letter that he wrote to Sir R. Maxwell in 1943, "which is better, to take the opponent's life secretly or openly, or to credit him with finer feelings and evoke them by fasting and the like? Again, which is better, to trifle with one's own life by fasting or some other means of self-immolation, or to trifle with it by engaging in an attempt to compass the destruction of the opponent and his dependents?"[46] The above reply shows that in situations where there are chances of violence and there seems no way out for the change to be brought about in the opponent, fasting may be resorted to as the only available non-violent means. It is really the outbreak of violence which is to be guarded against. Fasting reduces or rather removes all such chances of violence and therefore as a technique of nonviolent resistance it may be sometimes resorted to against the opponent also. As in the case of *ahimsā*, we saw, there may be exceptions in situations of moral dilemma, similarly in case of fasting also, there may be exceptions that must be left to the discretion of the *satyāgrahi* who has been well-trained and disciplined in the science of *Satyāgraha* and who understands and knows the demand of the situation. Gandhi was fully alive to the risks involved in fasting as a method of *Satyāgraha*. This is why he always insisted on its being used very sparingly, and only by those who had mastered the science of *Satyāgraha*.

Such charges of veiled or indirect coercion might be brought also against Gandhi's weapons of civil disobedience and non-cooperation. It might be said that by adopting the methods of civil disobedience and non-cooperation Gandhi in a way forced the Govt. to act contrary to its wishes, and therefore it amounted to pressure and coercion. Gandhi's reply to such charges of coercion would be that true coercion always implies violence, and because no act of violence was involved in civil disobedience and non-cooperation, no real coercion was being exerted against the Government. There was no question of moral impropriety in disobeying the State, because people were not bound to observe the tyrannical and immoral laws of the State." Civil disobedience did not presuppose lawlessness, rather it was based on a willing observance of all laws which did not hurt the moral sense or violate individual conscience. A true observance of civil disobedience demanded a law-abiding spirit combined with utmost self-restraint."[47] In this sense, civil disobedience, according to Gandhi, was the purest type of constitutional agitation. Of course, as he said, "it becomes degrading and despisable if its civil, i.e., non-violent character is a mere camouflage."[48] Similarly, there is no sense of coercion or immorality about non-cooperation also, if one understood its true nature and spirit. Behind non-cooperation, there is always the keenest desire of co-operation, provided the State or the authority concerned showed even the least sign of sympathy and consideration. As Gandhi very clearly said, "Behind my non-cooperation, there is always the keenest desire to cooperate on the slightest pretext even with the worst of opponents. To me, a very imperfect mortal, ever in need of God's grace, no one is beyond redemption."[49] So charges of coercion and constraint cannot be validly sustained against Gandhi's civil disobedience and non-cooperation if they are understood in a proper perspective.

We have seen that a true observance of *Satyāgraha* requires a strict discipline on the part of the *Satyāgrahi*. He has to fulfil certain conditions to be a *Satyāgrahi* in the true sense. Gandhi. laid down several such conditions. For example, a *Satyāgrahi* should be completely free from anger, hatred, lust, pride, fear and such other vices. He must "reduce himself to zero" and have perfect control over his senses. Besides, he must be honest, submissive and always ready to suffer. Most of all, he must have a strong faith in God or Truth. It is really this faith which sustains the *Satyāgrahi* in hours of excessive torture and suffering. He is also required to have complete trust in his soul-force as well as in the reform ability and convertibility of his opponent. For this he must believe that the opponent also has a soul in his being and reality of which he and his opponent are one. As Gandhi said very significantly in accordance with his deep-rooted trust in the divinity of man and in the unity of all existence, "Even if the opponent plays him false twenty times, the *satyāgrahi* is ready to trust him the twenty-first time, for an implicit trust in human nature is the very essence of his creed."[50] If one does not believe in the inner goodness of man, one cannot be a *satyāgrahi*. This is the basic metaphysical, psychological, and moral condition of *satyāgraha*.

In strict conformity with the Indian tradition channelized through Hinduism, Buddhism and Jainism, Gandhi took the *Panchamahāvrtas* (as it is called in Jainism) as essential moral vows to be observed by every man, and specially by a *satyāgrahi*. These are—*satya, ahimsā, brahmacharya, asteya* and *aparigraha*. *Satya* and *ahimsā*, as we have already seen, constitute the very essence of *Satyāgraha*. But, as we have also seen, for a real pursuit of Truth and a true observance of *ahimsā*, complete non-possession and control over the senses are also necessary. In other words, for a true observance of *ahimsā* in the pursuit of Truth, the observance of the virtues of *brahmachaya*, *asteya* and *aparigraha* are necessary. *Asteya* and *aparigraha* can both be seen simultaneously for all practical purpose, because both of them are concerned broadly with non-possession, which in Gandhi's conception means not having or willing to have in one's possession, things more than what are required for satisfying the minimum needs of a man as a physical being. Complete non-possession is an ideal which cannot be fulfilled so long as man has an ephemeral body. '*Asteya*' literally means non-stealing, i.e., not taking things belonging to others without their consent. But considered broadly, *asteya* implies not possessing material things disproportionate to one's requirements. And here it comes very close to *aparigraha*. So Gandhi has mainly laid emphasis upon non-possession as a condition for a follower of *ahimsā* or *satyāgraha*. For inculcating the virtue of love in its true spirit, non-possession is necessary. So long as one does not give up lust for possession, he will not be able to renounce selfishness and so he cannot love others in the true sense. So, for a *Satyāgrahi* the observance of the vow of non-possession is necessary. The ideal is complete non-possession, but as it is not possible practically, Gandhi advised minimum of possession which could satisfy the minimum essential needs of the body. All these ideas of Gandhi reflect not only the impact of Hinduism, Buddhism and Jainism upon him, but also of Christianity in which poverty or non-possession has been regarded as a condition for spiritual growth as well as for cultivating true love with one's fellow beings and God. The Sermon on the Mount declared that it is the poor and the meek who will attain the kingdom of God; they, therefore, are blessed.

Besides non-possession, the virtue which according to Gandhi must be cultivated by a *satyāgrahi* is what has been generally known as *brahmacharya* in the Indian tradition. '*Brahmacharya*' literally means the discipline or the way of life which leads to *Brahma* or God. Gandhi defined '*Brahmacharya*' as "that conduct which puts one in touch with God,"[51] and further pointed out The conduct consists in the fullest in this connection that control over all the senses. Popularly it has come to mean mere physical control over the organ of generation. This narrow meaning has debased *Brahmacharya* and made its practice all but impossible. Control over the organ of generation is impossible without proper control over the senses "..... *Brahmacharya* must be observed in thought, word and deed."[52] Thus *brahmacharya* according to Gandhi means an overall control on the senses and such a control must be brought about not forcibly on the physical plane merely, but also on the plane of thought by gradually taming and saddling the mind. This kind of control over the senses is necessary for a *satyāgrahi*.

Brahmacharya forms the first *āshrama* of the *āshrama*-system of Hinduism. It refers to the life-stage of studentship which requires a life of celibacy, complete control over the senses and total devotion to the acquisition of knowledge at the feet of the *Guru*. This life of studentship has no social obligations to discharge and it is a pre-marriage stage of life. Evidently, therefore, the virtue or vow of *brahmacharya* which Gandhi referred to as a necessary vow to be observed by a *satyāgrahi* is different from the *brahmachary āshram* of the Hindu *āshrama* system. For, if not so, then only people at the *brahmacharya* stage of life could be *Satyāgrahis*, which is not really the case. Gandhi himself was a married man and was always be seized with social obligations, but still he was an ideal *satyāgrahi*. This shows that although the qualities of a *brahmachari*, specially the qualities of charity, celibacy and the control of senses, are to be inculcated by a *satyāgrahi*; he need not be at the *brahmacharya* stage of life. Actually, if we try to understand the nature of the kind of life a *Satyāgrahi* should follow in terms of the four stages of the *āshrama* system of Hinduism, it must be the life of *vānaprastha* according to Gandhi. Gandhi himself liked this label to be applied to the kind of life he led. In other words, he liked himself to be called a *Vānaprasthin*. People so often called him a sage, an ascetic or a *sāñyasi*, but Gandhi did not like such labels for himself, because he wanted to devote himself to the service of the society and the stage of *sannayāsa* is, in the Hindu *āshrama*-system, a stage of the renunciation of the social bonds. Gandhi did not want to be free from social bonds, although he was ready to be free from all kinds of possessions, all kinds of wordily attractions and all kinds of selfish and sensual bonds. With all these considerations in view, the life of a *vānaprasthin* suited to him most and that kind of life he took to be the ideal for a *Satyāgrahi*. Much of the discipline meant for the *brahmacharya* stages of life tallies with that of the *vānaprastha* stage, except that a *vanaprasthin* is not a student and he is not without a wife and children, although he is no longer attached to them in any narrow selfish bond. According to Manu, a *vānaprasthin* must control his mind and senses, be free from any lust for possession, be charitable, chaste, patient, friendly, and compassionate towards all creatures.[53] He may commit his wife to his sons or may, if she so likes, allow her to accompany him. ?[54] When Gandhi took the *brahmacharya* vow with the consent of his wife, he really did so with a view to entering into the stage of *vānaprastha*. So, according to him, the life of *vānaprastha* is the ideal life for a *satyāgrahi*, This life, according to Gandhi, is free from family obligations, but is not free from wider social obligations. So it gives an occasion for wider and truer commitment to Truth and *ahimsā*. In this life of *vānaprastha*, Gandhi did not cut off all connections from his wife, rather allowed her to accompany him on many occasions, but then with her consent he gave up all sexual connections with her. Although, as we have said above, Gandhi did not mean by *brahmacharya* only giving up sexual intercourse, but then he much emphasized upon it as being a necessary condition for anyone to be a true *Satyāgrahi*. Gandhi did not hate sexual intercourse under legitimate married relationship, but then, quite in conformity with the Hindu *Shāstras*, he advised to take to sexual intercourse only with the intention of having a child. Because at the *vānasprastha* stage, such a desire is not (or should not be) there, one should not take to sexual intercourse at this stage. Moreover, according to Gandhi, renunciation of sex gives stamina and firmness of purpose by conserving vital energy and this provides the *Satyāgrahi* with the capacity of firm determination, which he so urgently requires. So, Gandhi was very firmly opposed to *satyāgrahis* being wedded to sexual relationship. He did not advise giving up the company of women; women could very well be in the company of *satyāgrahis*. But one must have to treat them as mothers and sisters. Even married couple, if they were to become *satyāgrahis*, must treat each other as brother and sister. This aspect of Gandhi's thought may seem to some as quite unnatural and ridiculous, but this is what he believed in and for himself he firmly stuck to also throughout his *satyāgrahi* career. Gandhi was also of faith that only complete renunciation of sex could lead one to Truth or God. Besides, sex, Gandhi also advised abstention from intoxicating drinks and drugs for a *satyāgrahi*. All these reflect a very great influence upon him of the Hindu *Dharma-sutrās* and *Dharma-shāstrās* which he sometimes also criticized in so far as they upheld the vice of untouchability.

Thus, we can see that although *satyāgraha* proved in the hands of Gandhi to be a weapon of great social and political changes, it was basically a religious concept based on inspirations drawn from Hindu, Buddha, Jaina and Christian religious traditions. Therefore, it may be said that many who criticized *satyāgraha* were really criticizing the intrusion of religion into politics. But Gandhi was firm to the innermost depth of his heart on the point that politics without religion was simply a lifeless corpse worth nothing.

(D) SARVODAYA

The word '*Sarvodaya*' is a compound of two words '*sarva*' (All) and '*udaya*' (Welfare or upliftment). Thus, it means welfare or upliftment of all. According to Gandhi, it is *sarvodaya*, i. e,, the good or the welfare of all, which should be the aim of all human activities. It is our highest end, the *summum bonum*. The good or the welfare aimed at is the all-round welfare-social, political, economic, etc., and it is the good not only of men but also of animals and even of the natural world. In this, Gandhi significantly differs from the viewpoint of the utilitarians like Mill, according to whom, the aim of our actions should be the greatest good of the greatest number. Gandhi could never subscribe to such a view that we should always care for the majority only. The minority which was left out of the preview of such views was really his main concern. In the light of his philosophy of *Advaita* he believed in the unity of all existence and consequently in the unity and equality of all men. So, he wondered how could we aim at the good of a few only, leaving aside others, even if the latter might be in a sheer minority. Gandhi really never believed in the philosophy that, if by some of our actions the majority gained, our purpose was fulfilled. He, on the contrary, believed that even if one man suffered, our purpose was defeated and we proved failure. Men were all essentially one and therefore, it was not conceivable how others could gain while even one suffered. As Gandhi said, "I do not believe that an individual may gain spiritually and those that surrounded him suffer. I believe in advaita. I believe in the essential unity of man and for that matter of all that lives. Therefore, I believe that if one man gains spiritually, the whole world gains with him and, if one man falls, the whole world falls to that extent."[55] Thus the ideal of *sarvodaya* which Gandhi so fervently cherished was really contained in the philosophy of man that he believed in. We have seen in his philosophy of man in our earlier chapter and have found that according to him every man has a soul within him which is really the light of God within him. In this being of the soul or *Ātman*, men are all essentially one, because they partake of the same reality or Truth. As Gandhi very clearly said, "I believe in absolute oneness of God and therefore also of humanity. What though we have many bodies? We have but one soul. The rays of the sun are many through refraction. But they have the same source."[56] Hence, *sarvodaya* seems to be the logical outcome of the metaphysical beliefs of Gandhi regarding the nature of man and God.

From a different angle, the concept of *sarvodaya* seems to be a direct outcome of Gandhi's philosophy of Truth and *ahimsā*. We have seen that Gandhi took Truth as the end and *ahimsā* the means. By truth he actually meant God himself and as God is absolutely one, Truth is also absolutely one. But there are various refractions or manifestations of God or Truth, every one of which represents Truth in its own partial way. None is to be regarded as more or less valuable in comparison with the others.

All are equally valuable or equally true. Therefore, the welfare or good of all should be our necessary concern. And that can be achieved only through the path of self-suffering, self-sacrifice and universal love, which are all the ingredients of *ahimsā*. Thus a votary of *ahimsā* cannot but pursue the ideal of *sarvodaya*, because his love for every one of God's manifestation will compel him to work for the good of all. We have seen that Truth and *ahimsā* according to Gandhi are like the two sides of the same coin and the realization of Truth can never be possible without the path of *ahimsā*. Thus a lover of Truth will naturally be a lover of *ahimsā* and the combined result of the two pursuits will be the good of all–*Sarvodaya*. A seeker after truth and a votary of *ahimsā* cannot work for the good of a few, leaving aside others. Deciphering the nature of his idea of *sarvodaya* by distinguishing it from the narrower utilitarian ideal, Gandhi himself remarked, "A votary of *ahimsā* cannot subscribe to the utilitarian formula (of the greatest good of the greatest number). He will strive for the greatest good of all and will die in the attempt to realize the ideal. He will therefore be willing to die, so that others may live. He will serve himself with the rest, by himself dying. The greatest good of all inevitably includes the good of the greatest number, and therefore, he and the utilitarian will converge in many points in their career but there does come a time when they must part company, and even work in opposite directions. The utilitarian to be logical will never sacrifice himself. The absolutist will even sacrifice himself."[57] The last two sentences clearly indicate that the path of a *sarvodayi* is necessarily the path of *ahimsā* of pure love, suffering and sacrifice for the sake of others, but the path of an utilitarian is not so.

In fact, the utilitarian theory is out and out a consequentialist or teleological theory of morality in which what counts is the end, the goal. The means does not at all matter. The greatest good of the greatest number is the ideal and that is to be achieved by whatever means possible. But we know that for Gandhi means and end were inseparable and a good end according to him could be achieved only by adopting a good means. Ahimsā or love therefore was the only means according to him through which the ideal of *sarvodaya* could be pursued and achieved. Gandhi preached *sarvodaya* to be the end of all our actions, but he was not a consequentialist out and out. The end was always related according to him to the path that one adopted. This speaks of the vital difference between the Gandhian ideal of *sarvodaya* and the utilitarian ideal of the greatest good of the greatest number. Moreover, while the ideal of sarvodaya is definitely based on an essentially spiritualistic outlook regarding world and man, the utilitarian ideal seems to be based on a rational and social consideration and has for its metaphysical basis a materialistic outlook, because the good that it envisages as the end to be pursued is for the most part, the material good. The end that Gandhi aimed at was, on the other hand, the spiritual good, the spiritual welfare of man, although it did not exclude the material good.

As a matter of fact, Gandhi's *sarvodaya* aimed at an all-round development of man as a whole. This all-round development or welfare included within it man's social, political, economic and spiritual development all taken together. It was with this aim that Gandhi always worked hard for the social upliftment of the down-trodden like the *shudrās* or the untouchables and the women. His whole social lite as a matter of fact was devoted to the upliftment and welfare of these two classes which were most neglected and suppressed. In the true spirit of his doctrine of *sarvodaya*, Gandhi felt that so long as one considerable portion of humanity remained down-trodden and suffering, the welfare of all could not even be dreamt of. It was really with this ideal of *sarvodaya* in view, that Gandhi fought for the freedom of the Indian people. But again, although freedom of the Indian people was his immediate concern, he really fought for the freedom of all those who were subjected to unjust rule and tyranny. As a matter of fact, Gandhi took State as such as an inherent evil, so far as the development of each individual man was concerned. He was in favour of the least possible powers to be given to the State and at last he favoured a State-less society in which every man could live free and independent according to his will and conscience. Undue interference of the state in individual liberty, Gandhi never tolerated. Similarly, Gandhi always fought for the economic freedom of the poor and the needy. He always preached equitable distribution of property and wealth so that the poorest and the most neglected could get their due share. Gandhi believed that no spiritual development of man was possible without his economic freedom. For a starving man it was the bread which was real God. The following words of Gandhi will make his meaning very clear in this regard, "I may as well place before the dogover there the message of God as before those hungry millions who have no lustre in their eyes and whose only God is bread."[58] Gandhi took it to be our moral duty to help the poor in improving their economic condition. Our unity with all our fellowmen made it obligatory upon us that we helped them by curtailing our own needs and demands. We must adjust our wants and undergo voluntary sacrifice for the sake of the poor. Religion consisted for Gandhi, as we have seen even earlier, not in seeking one's own salvation in seclusion, but in helping the helpless and working for the poor and the needy. Gandhi's passion to serve the poor and the unprivileged was so great that he claimed to find God not in temples and mosques but in the hearts of the poor. As he said, "I am endeavouring to see God through the service of humanity, for I know that God is neither in heaven nor down below, but in everyone."[59] To give food to the hungry was, for Gandhi, like giving gift to God. Without helping the poor to rise above their miserable conditions, it was not possible for Gandhi to realise the Truth or God. This idea is also reflected in his view that religion and morality are very intimately related and that without, or apart from, morality there could be no religion. Religion consists mainly in one's effort for realizing God or Truth and we have seen that for Gandhi the most effective means for doing so is *ahimsā* which implies within it the moral qualities of love, self-sacrifice and suffering for the sake of others.

We have seen that by '*Sarvodaya*' Gandhi meant all-round development or upliftment of all. Here by 'all', he meant not only the human class, but also the sub-human sphere of existence including animals, plants, etc. as well as the inanimate nature. And this was in perfect consistency with his fundamental belief in the unity of all existence. It was due to this belief that he always preached and practised sincere love for even "the meanest of creation as oneself." He had a genuine feeling of affinity with the entire animal life and it was a symbol of this feeling that he praised the custom of cow-protection or cow-worship that is prevalent amongst the Hindus. He took cow in this context as a representative of animal life and said that Hindu cow-worship was really a symbol of the Hindu belief that animal life was as much valuable as the human one.

Gandhi was totally opposed to the killing animals for the purpose of food. He therefore always took vegetarian diet. It is a fact, he conceded, that even in the vegetables and plants there was life and therefore in taking them for food or in destroying them for other purposes, we commit *himsā*. But, as we have seen earlier, Gandhi also conceded that as far as we had a physical body, we could not resort to complete *ahimsā*. Nevertheless, this practical difficulty never shook his absolute faith in *ahimsā* and his own life is an example of how one should practise *ahimsā* to his maximum capacity even in spite of certain practical difficulties. He always insisted that there was a fundamental difference between an outlook of life which was based on the principle of *ahimsā* and love and that which was based on the principle of *himsā* and hatred. And this difference could not be removed or blurred by the fact that even a follower of *ahimsā* has sometimes to resort to some amount of *himsā* out of unavoidable practical necessity. Gandhi had a genuine feeling of love not only for the animal life but also for the inanimate nature and it was in perfect consonance with this feeling that he expressed his disapproval of the excessive exploitation of nature by the modern industrial and technological society. The technological advance of the modern Western world is so often attributed to the Christian faith that God commanded Adam to rule over the entire nature including the animal realm, because he (Adam) and through him the entire human race was taken by God as the master of creation. To this Gandhi would perhaps say that this is a misinterpretation of the Christian faith, because God's command did never imply an unqualified, merciless exploitation of nature. Nature is as dear to God as anything else.

In the light of the above analysis of Gandhi's concept of *sarvodaya*, it may be said that if this is all that he meant by *sarvodaya*, then certainly it is nothing but an utopian ideal which could never be achieved. Gandhi would perhaps never have much objection to such a remark except that he would certainly not like the adjective 'utopian'. *Sarvodaya* is of course an ideal, and ideals are after all ideals which are not necessarily to be achieved in full. What is important regarding ideals is that we must make sincere efforts for them, we must strive after them. Gandhi could not appreciate the force of the argument that because something was not easily achievable, it must not serve as our ideal. According to him, on the other hand, our ideal must be very high, it must be in consonance with our true nature and the nature of God or Truth. If our ideal is high and we make sincere effort for it, our job is finished. As Gandhi said, "Let us be sure of our ideal. We shall ever fail to realize it but should never cease to strive for it."[60] At another place he said in a similar vein, "The goal ever recedes from us. The greater the progress the greater the recognition of our unworthiness. Satisfaction lies in the effort, not in the attainment. Full effort is full victory."[61] Our aim must be *sarvodaya,* because nothing short of that will be logically consistent with our true nature. Whether we shall be able to achieve that goal perfectly or not is immaterial. Gandhi believed with Newman that if a man stooped even one step further towards the realization of his goal, that was enough for him. Gandhi's ideal of *sarvodaya* seems to have a near affinity with the Christian idea of the kingdom of God, by the realization of which God's purpose will be completely fulfilled and everyone will live in a reign of perfect love and brotherliness with all aspects of natural, animal and human life. Again, in counselling to work ceaselessly for one's ideal whether it is achieved or not, Gandhi seems to be guided by the same spirit of *nishkāma karma* of the *Gitā* by which he was guided throughout his life. We must keep our ideal high and work hard for that. The result is in the hands of God, ours part is simply to work *(Karmanye vādhi kā raste, māphaleshu kadāchana).*

Although, it can be said undoubtedly that in formulating his concept of *sarvodaya* Gandhi was influenced by all such sources which influenced him in his formulation of the concepts of *Satya* and *ahimsā,* he was mainly influenced in this regard by his own religious and philosophical tradition. In other words, although religious like Buddhism, Christianity etc. played a vital role in strengthening the ideas of self-sacrifice, universal brotherhood, selfless service etc. in Gandhi, mainly it is the deep-rooted Hindu beliefs and ideas in him which made him a true votary of the ideal of *sarvodaya.* It was a logical demand of the philosophy of Advaita that he should advocate and work for the welfare, the good and the upliftment of all. If the entire existence was basically one, we could have neither any basis nor any justification for aiming at the good of a certain number only, leaving aside others. As a matter of fact, we could not do it at all because all were bound by the same spiritual string. In this he was clearly echoing the spirit of the following ancient Sanskrit verse—*Sarvebhawantusukhinah sarvesantu nirāmayah; Sarve bhadrāni pash yantu, mā kaschiddukhama pruyata.* Besides this and many other verses from the *Upanishads* and the Gita that influenced Gandhi in formulating his concept of *sarvodaya*, it was the following very first verse of the *Ishopanishad* which had the greatest impact upon him—*Isāvāsyamidam sarvam Yatkincha jagatyām jagat; tena tyaktena bhun ithāmā grdhatik-asyasvit dharam* (whatever exists in this changing universe, all that is embraced by the Lord: enjoy by renouncing it; covet not anybody's wealth). Thus whatever is there in the universe is pervaded by God. God is present in everything and everything is his. Taking this as the basic truth, one should realize the essential unity of the entire universe and learn the lesson of renunciation and sacrifice. Because everything is God's, we should cultivate a spirit of complete detachment and work for the good of others. This is the essential teaching of the *Gitā* and as a matter of fact of all the religions of the world. We have seen that self-sacrifice, working for the good of others and cultivating a spirit of universal love are the essentials of *sarvodaya* and all these are basically contained in this single verse. Gandhi himself was very much appreciative of this verse and said that there was nothing essential of any religion which was left out of this verse. To quote his own words in this connection, "I have in my search of the scriptures of the world found nothing to add to this mantra. Looking back upon all the little I have read of the scriptures..... I feel that everything good in all the scriptures is derived from this mantra. If it is universal brotherhood—not only brotherhood of all human beings, but of all living beings-I find it in this mantra. If it is the idea of complete surrender to God and of the faith that he will supply all that I need, then again, I say, I find it in this mantra. Since he pervades every fibre of..... being and of all of you, I derive from it the doctrine of equality of all creatures Of earth and it should satisfy the cravings of all philosophical communists. This mantra tells me that I cannot hold as mine anything that belongs to God, and if my life and that of all who believe in this mantra has to be a life of perfect dedication, it follows that it will have to be a life of continual service of all our fellow-creatures."[62] It may seem to many that Gandhi has given rather a very inflated status to the verse and has added much more meaning to it from his own side than it actually has.

But if one goes deep into the meaning of the verse, one may see that none of the derivations that Gandhi has made is either stipulated or concocted or is a sign of his wishful thinking. Because God pervades everything or, in other words, because God is present in everything, there is no real distinction between myself and others. Universal brotherhood, therefore, is the natural consequence. Then again, because everything belongs to God, or in other words, because he is the master of everything, complete surrender to him and a perfectly detached attitude with a readiness to work for the good of others will be the most rational attitude. Furthermore, because God is all-pervading, the doctrine of the equality of all creatures naturally follows. Then again, because everything belongs to God, renunciation, *aparigraha* and non-covetousness become the natural moral consequences. Thus Gandhi's claims about the verse are neither inflated nor stipulated. The verse really contains in a nut-shell all the essentials of a religion and the most potent seed of *sarvodaya*.

It is clear from the above that Gandhi's essentially Hindu background and his study of the various Hindu scriptures had already sowed the seed of *sarvodaya* in his heart, but the most imminent impetus for formulating his idea of *sarvodaya* in a concrete form, Gandhi seems to have got from his study of Ruskin's small book *Unto The Last*. In this book Gandhi found an echo of his views that were taking shape in him by the help of his Hindu ideas and beliefs. He translated the book in Gujarati with the title *Sarvodaya* and summarised the main teachings of the book under the following three headings:

1. The good of the individual is contained in the good of all.
2. A lawyer's work has the same value as that of a barber in that all men have the same right to earn a living from their labour.
3. A life of labour in which one works with his own hands is the life worth living.

As a matter of fact, it is these three principles which served as the foundation of Gandhi's concept of *sarvodaya*. We can see that the first principle enunciated here is nothing but a reflection of the same basic spiritual conviction of Gandhi, according to which there is a basic unity amongst all creatures. When all are basically one, there is no real question of mine and thine and thus there is no question of serving one's own interest apart from the interest of others. Naturally, therefore, one's own good is associated with the good of all. One cannot gain separately in complete isolation from others. We have seen Gandhi expressing his view clearly that if one man gains spiritually, all others also gain to that extent and if one man loses, all others also lose. If this be a fact, then it is quite clear that there is no individual gain or loss apart from the gain or loss of the entire human race, or, as a matter of fact, of the entire creation. This is really the basic truth upon which the whole philosophy of *sarvodaya* is based and in this respect, it can be seen that *sarvodaya* is a logical consequence of man's true nature. In a world where all are basically one, none can be able to serve his own real interest, unless he serves the interest of all.

The second principle reflects Gandhi's firm conviction in the *Gitā* ideal of *svadharma*. Whatever status one has got in the society by virtue of his *varna* or qualities of action, he has to work in accordance with that. There is no question of any one's work being superior or inferior to that of the other. All works have got their own value and therefore all are equally valuable. Thus we can see that the second principle is based on a conviction in the principle of the dignity of labour. The value of the fruit of labour, of whatever kind or status it may be, cannot be minimized or ignored. Every kind of labour sincerely carried out has got its own dignity and the work of a barber can in no way be treated as inferior to the work of a lawyer.

The third principle clearly reflects Gandhi's love for those who perform manual labour and who are generally the down-trodden, the poor and the hungry in the society. In a way, here again is reflected Gandhi's love and regard for labourers, tillers, farmers etc, who do physical labour but remain the most neglected and the most suppressed in the society. It is with a view to giving high status to the manual labourers that Gandhi developed the concept of bread-labour, which we shall see in our subsequent pages. The concept of *Sarvodaya,* no doubt, implies the upliftment and good of all, as we have been seeing all along, but the upliftment of the down-trodden, the poor, the neglected, was Gandhi's primary concern and this he wanted to convey through his principle of *sarvodaya* also. *Sarvodaya* implies the development of all, but it first and foremost implies the development of all those who need it most. As a matter of fact, Gandhi worked for his whole life for the upliftment of the poor and the down-trodden.

The ideal of *sarvodaya* may in certain respects be compared to the ideal envisaged by socialism and communism in so far as the latter also like the former talk of the equality of all men and advocate the need for providing them equal opportunities and equal share of all economic goods etc. Gandhi himself made such a scope for comparison between *sarvodaya* and what he called philosophical communism while he was analysing the aspects of *sarvodaya* involved in the mantra of the *Ishopanishad* quoted above. But there is a fundamental difference between *sarvodaya* on the one hand and socialism and communism on the other. The former has for its necessary basis the spiritual unity of all beings which Gandhi so fervently believed in, while the latter have no such basis because they stand only on certain material and social considerations. It is really by keeping in view this spiritualistic background of *saryodaya* that Jay Prakash Narayan remarked in his book *Samājvāda, Sarvodaya Aur Lokatantra* that unless socialism was converted into *sarvodaya,* its high ideals of freedom, equality, brotherhood, world peace etc. would remain always beyond its reach. [63] For want of the sound spiritual basis which really becomes the philosophical basis for all such ideals, the ideals will remain merely high slogans. Unless one realizes within his heart the inner affinity and unity of all beings, he cannot work from within for the equality and upliftment of all. Spiritualism of *sarvodaya* provides a sound basis for all socialistic or communistic efforts. Furthermore, the ideal of *sarvodaya* is essentially to be achieved through the path of *ahimsā,* while the ideals of socialism or communism do not necessarily admit of the path of *ahimsā*. The communists rather have openly preached the necessity of the path of *himsā* for bringing about social equality.

Philosophers of the world have so often spoken of *Ātma-darshana* or *Ātma-bodha* (self-realization or self-knowledge) to be the ultimate aim or end of man's life. Our *Upanishads* speak of '*Ātmānam Viddihih*', Socrates exhorted 'know thyself' and the famous Danish thinker Kierkegaard sounds the same Socratic note in modern times in his own existentialist way. Gandhi's ideal of *sarvodaya* also involves within it an element of the ideal of *ātma-bodha* or *ātma-dhashana* within it. Gandhi said that *sarvodaya* was the highest end of man's life. He also said that self-realization or the realization of God was our highest end.

There seems to be an apparent discrepancy between these two statements. *Sarvodaya* and Self-realization apparently seem to be two completely different ideals and it is not clear how one can take both of them together to be the highest end of life?

But if we go somewhat deeper into Gandhi's concepts of *sarvodaya* and self-realization, we will find that the imagined separating line between the two begins to vanish and the two ideals converge. Self-realization, according to Gandhi, does not mean finding out some such unique reality within oneself which is separate from all else in the universe. Furthermore, it is not to be found in isolation from others by the path of *nivrtti*. The self is one with God and God is one with the entire universe and so self-realization means realization of God and that in its turn means realization of all within one's own being. In other words. when one realizes that the barrier between himself and the entire universe is just an imaginary one and that all are basically one, he has realized his self and has attained what is called *ātma-bodha*. Hence *ātma-bodha*, according to Gandhi, as according to Tagore and Vivakanand also, means seeing or finding oneself into others and others into oneself. And this is really the ideal of *Sarvoday a*also. To see one'sinterest being realized through the interest of others is to be filled with the sense of *sarvodaya*. To realize others in one-self and oneself in others is the first lesson of *sarvodaya*. Again, working for *sarvodaya* and working for self-realization are also one and the same thing. Both can be attained, according to Gandhi, by adopting the path of complete *ahimsā,* universal love and brotherhood and selfless social service. It is through the *tapasyā* of *ahimsā* and selfless love for others, and not through any *tapasyā* in the jungle, that self-realization or God-realization is possible according to Gandhi.

And the same is needed for the attainment of the ideal of *sarvodaya* also. Hence, properly understood, the ideals of self-realization or *sarvodaya* do not remain two distinct ideals, rather they converge more or less on the same point. It is in course of writing in this spirit that Jay Prakash Narayan has said that the very foundation of morality consists in realizing this fundamental unity amongst all beings which may be called self-realization also. [64]

It may still be pointed out that the above kind of affinity between the ideals of *sarvodaya* and self-realization have been brought about by means of a muddling of the two concepts. Some of the very obvious differences between the two cannot be ruled out in the above manner. It may be said, for example, that whereas *sarvodaya* is a social and ethical ideal, self-realization is a spiritual and religious ideal. Furthermore, it may be said that *sarvodaya* can at most be the means for the end of self-realization and both cannot be ends at the same time. In other words, it can be said, if we work for the upliftment or welfare of all (i.e. *sarvodaya*), then perhaps through that means we can realize our self. Taken in this sense, *sarvodaya* becomes the means and self-realization the end. It cannot be said point-blank that there is no point in such arguments, but we would like to submit here that if we try to understand Gandhi's standpoint somewhat more closely by bringing about certain facts about his thought which we have already referred to earlier, we can see that there is an important sense in which we can take the ideals of *sarvodaya* and self-realization as one and the same ideal, differently understood from different standpoints. Even if it is taken for granted that *sarvodaya* is only the means and self-realization the end, no discrepancy is created in Gandhi's thought, because we know that, according to him, means and end are convertible terms, the two sides of the same coin, and there is no absolute distinction between the two. Self-realization as end is nothing different from the means of working for *sarvodaya,* because it is in and through this working that one's self is truly realized. If we have begun working for the upliftment of all with the inner realization that all of us are basically one, we have realized our self. Self-realization is nothing over and above the true working for the upliftment and good of all. Similarly, the distinction between social and ethical ideal on the one hand and spiritual and religious ideal on the other does not hold good in the context of Gandhian thought. We have seen that according to Gandhi there can be no religion without morality; true religion consists in nothing but serving humanity with a sense of inner love and compassion. Any spiritual ideal can be realized only in and through the social and moral service, and not by a *tapasyā* in the jungle. A life of *ahimsā* and love sincerely carried out is the real life of *tapasyā* according to Gandhi.

It is in the context of the above ideas of Gandhi that one can see the utter failure of the criticism so often levelled against Hindu thought and religion that it is other-worldly and has no place for social service etc. in the realization of *Moksha*. Gandhi has shown that essentially the spiritual ideal of self-realization or *Moksha* is nothing different from the social ideal of *Sarvodaya*. And as the latter is to be achieved clearly by adopting the path of social service, mutual love and compassion, so the former also is attainable by the self-same means. With a view to highlight the superiority of Christianity over Hinduism and Buddhism, Paul Tillich, the great American theologian, has more recently made a distinction between them on the ground that "while within the Christian concept of *agape* or love it is possible for man to remove his alienation or estrangement from the ground of Being by means of his participation in the community and social life through love and compassion, it is not possible in the context of Hindu or Buddha religions as they fail to give us a means of participation in the social life through similar human virtues."[65]But we can see now very clearly how ill-conceived such distinctions are. One can hardly resent the absence of social life or a life of community based on the virtues of mutual love and brotherhood in Hinduism and Buddhism if he honestly goes through and tries to understand the above ideas of Gandhi which, although influenced in their various aspects by the various religions of the world, are pre-eminently and basically a product of his Hindu heritage along with the added impact of the two allied religions, Buddhism and Jainism. In Buddhism it is more glaringly visible in the life of the Sangha, which forms one of the pillars of the famous *Trisaranagamanam* known also as the three jewels of Buddhism. In Hinduism also, the life of community based on the human virtues of *ahimsā, aparigraha* etc. has always been emphasized as forming an essential component of the path towards salvation. The path of *Niskāma Karma* so importantly envisaged in the Hindu sacred text *Bhagavad-Gitā* and also in other such texts bears ample testimony to the Hindu concern for a life of community based on selfless social service and love. Gandhi's identification of *Sarvodaya* with self-realization is a result of all such elements present in Hinduism, Buddhism and Jainism.

(E) SWARĀJ

The term '*Swarāj*' literally means self-rule or self-government. It was apparently used by Gandhi as a term referring to the removal of the British rule from India and the installation of a national Government instead. On the face, *swarāj* in the above sense seems to have been the goal of Gandhi for which he adopted the various non-violent means, such as, non-co-operation, civil disobedience etc. But in fact, Gandhi used the term '*swarāj*' in a very broad sense of which, of course, the removal of British rule and formation of a national government formed inevitable part. He adopted this word from the *Vedās* and maintained in his conception of it its essential Vedic character. He himself said about it, "The word *Swarāj* is a sacred word, a Vedic word, meaning self-rule and self-restraint, and not freedom from all restraint which 'independence' often means."[66] Thus *swarāj* or self-rule meant for Gandhi not only rule of, or by, the self, i.e., one's own rule or government, but also rule over the self. To keep the senses within legitimate limits, to relinquish selfishness, to sacrifice the self for others, to live a life of interdependence with all fellow-brothers are some of the marks of true *swarāj* according to Gandhi. Self-control and self-discipline, self-awareness and self-respect are the true marks of *swarāj*. Thus it is basically a spiritual concept which is more related to internal discipline and rule than with more external freedom and external rule. External freedom is a necessary but not a sufficient condition of *swarāj*. For real *swarāj* rule over one's own self is necessary. As Gandhi very clearly said, "Government over the self is the truest *swarāj*. It is synonymous with *moksha* or salvation."[67] Thus *swarāj* for Gandhi was as high as *moksha*. It consisted for him in self-control. Rule over the self or self-control really means freeing the self from all shackles of narrow egoism so as to extend it to be identified with other selves. In that sense it is spiritual freedom or *moksha*. So by labouring day and night for the *swarāj* of India, Gandhi was really fighting for each and every individual to be free from all sorts of bondage and limitation. He was really trying for self-purification. As he declared, "I am not interested in freeing India merely from the English yoke. I am bent upon freeing India from any yoke whatsoever. I have no desire to exchange' king log for king stork'. Hence for me the movement of *swarāj* is a movement of self-purification."[68] From all these it is quite clear that Gandhi took *swarāj* not merely as a political concept, but also as a spiritual concept. Rather the spiritualistic contents of the concept seem to have captured his mind more prominently. The *swarāj* of his conception was meant not only for Indians but for the entire mankind. Fighting for the *swarāj* of India was an emblem for the *swarāj* of the people of the entire world.

However, political or external freedom was taken by Gandhi as a necessary precondition for inner freedom or *swarāj* in the spiritual sense. The British domination over India had really enslaved the Indians in their soul and spirit and they had thereby lost their sense of self-respect. The revival of a sense of self-respect was necessary in them so that they could work for real *swarāj*. However, this political freedom was to be won by them according to Gandhi, not by any violent means but by the means of complete non-violence, self-suffering, self-sacrifice and love. He openly declared, "True democracy or the *swarāj* of the masses can never come through untruthful and violent means, for the simple reason that the natural corollary to their use would be to remove all opposition through the suppression or extermination of the antagonists. That does not make for individual freedom. Individual freedom can have the fullest play only under a regime of unadulterated *ahimsā*."[69] He compared the use of force for the attainment of *swarāj* (self-government) to the planting of a noxious weed in the hope that it would produce rose. Swarāj, for Gandhi, in the ultimate analysis, was a spiritual goal, a goal of spiritual freedom for each individual and such a pious goal could not be achieved by adopting the wrong path of violence and hatred. Only the path of *ahimsā* and love could give political freedom, and ultimately the real freedom. Gandhi felt that the British were not to grant *swarāj* to Indians quite automatically on their own. That had to be won. But it was not to be won by violent force. What was necessary for that was the soul-force, the strength of self-suffering and self-sacrifice and firm determination and perseverance. Gandhi firmly believed that "If India adopted the doctrine of love as an active part of her religion and introduced it in her politics, *swarāj* would descend upon India from heaven". [70] The British rulers were not to be coerced.

They were rather to be persuaded by the force of love. Use of physical force could never bring true *swarāj* according to Gandhi. It must have been clear to us from Gandhi's conception of man, that he ascribed ontological priority to the individual man over society or State. Therefore, in his effort for the freedom of India also, he was really giving priority to the freedom of each individual. Emphasizing his preference for individual freedom he said, "The first step to *swarāj* lies in the individual. The greatest truth: 'As with the individual so with the universe' is applicable here as elsewhere."[71] The statement expresses the ancient Indian belief that man is the centre of the universe and that self-discovery could lead to the realization of the whole of the cosmic Truth, the *Brahman*. Gandhi did never take the *swarāj* of a nation to be anything different from the *swarāj* of each and every individual of that nation. He openly said, *"Swarāj* of a people means the sum total of the *swarāj* (self-rule) of individuals."[72] A nation is really free when every citizen in it, however mean and low he may be, feels that he is free and he has his say in the government of the nation. He said, "*Swarāj* for me means freedom for the meanest of my countrymen."[73] Again, " Mere withdrawal of the English is not independence. It means the consciousness in the average villager that he is the maker of his own destiny, he is his own legislator through his chosen representatives."[74] Gandhi does not seem to have ever been in favour of majority rule, which was according to him after all the rule of a few. He said, " Real *swarāj* will come not by acquisition of authority by a few but by the acquisition of the capacity by all to resist authority when it is abused."[75]Thus he wanted real power to be vested in the hands of people, all people, and not a selected few, "... to me Hind *Swarāj* is the rule of all people, is the rule of Justice."[76] Undoubtedly, he was totally averse to any kind of dictatorship. He was not simply for somehow substituting the British rule by Indian rule, of whatever nature it might be. He was rather a passionate votary of true individual freedom and he was never ready to sacrifice it at any cost. This is clear from his own words, " There is no freedom for India so long as one man, no matter how highly placed he may be, holds in the hollow of his hands the life, property and the honour of millions of human beings. It is an artificial, unnatural and un-civilised institution. The end of it is an essential preliminary to swarāj."[77] It was for the sake of individual freedom that in the last resort Gandhi took a Stateless society to be the ideal society. But then he realized that it was only an ideal which could perhaps never be actualised in practice. Nevertheless, only a society in which each individual was his own ruler, was the ideal society for him.

It may be pointed out here that howsoever Gandhi idealised the concept of *swarāj*, in practice his *swarāj* meant nothing more than the freedom of India from the British rule. At least apparently it is this goal for the achievement of which he struggled for almost the entire span of his life. This practical aspect of Gandhi's *swarāj* can be interpreted as nothing more than a kind of narrow nationalism which does not wholly fit in with his ideal of *sarvodaya*. The discrepancy in his thought on this account can be put in the following two points-(1) Gandhi fought for the political freedom of India alone, although there were many other nations which were serving under foreign rule, (2) Gandhi's struggle for the removal of the British from India went against his principle that all men were basically one. When all men were basically one, what difference did it make if the British ruled India? Working for the removal of the British implied a sense of hatred against them which could not be reconciled with the ideal of *sarvodaya*. That also went against his claim that he regarded the people of work alike irrespective of their caste, face, nationality etc. He showed a definite favour for his own countrymen which was a sign of narrow nationalism. But such criticisms against Gandhi are the results of a wrong perspective and a bad logic. The first criticism can very well be answered by the help of Gandhi's concept of *swadeshi*, which we will see in a detailed form in the next chapter. The answer can very well be given in Gandhi's own words, "I work for India's freedom because my *swadeshi* teaches me that being born in it and having inherited her culture, I am fitted to serve her and she has a prior claim to my service."[78] Gandhi's *swadeshi* also is sometimes interpreted as a mark of his narrow nationalism, but we will see in our analysis of the concept that, to quote Gandhi's own words, it is an 'acme of universal service'. [79] Furthermore, his fight for the freedom of India was just a symbol of universal fight for freedom, for the eradication of slavery and oppression on matter whatever they existed. A finite man like Gandhi could not have unlimited power and capacity to fight simultaneously for the freedom of the people of the entire world, but his freedom-struggle in India really symbolized the struggle for the freedom of people all over the world. Gandhi wanted to achieve *swarāj* for his own people simply with a view to arouse the sense of self-respect in them. Once they were free from the yoke of slavery, Gandhi would advise them not to work for their own selfish ends, but to die for the sake of the world at large. As he said, "My love, therefore, of nationalism or my idea of nationalism is that my country may become free, that if need be, the whole of the country may die, so that the human race may live. There is no room for race hatred here. Let that be our nationalism."[80] These lines make it clear that there was nothing like hatred in any sense in Gandhi's heart against the British people. He never hated people however mean they might be. If at all he hated, he hated systems-such systems which undermined the value and dignity of individual man. He had no objection if British people lived in India and participated in a government which was in the real sense people's government. In fact, on the ideal level, he was in favour of no government in a centralised form, whether it be foreign or national. He wanted each individual to be his own ruler. Thus there is no question of his principle of *sarvodaya* and *ahimsā* being jeopardised by his call to remove British rule from India. The rule was unjust and racial in nature and it was in the true spirit of *sarvodaya* that Gandhi fought for the removal of such unjust rule. No individual or race has a right to dominate over other against the wishes or the interest of the latter. Because the Indian people were oppressed, it was the demand of the Gandhian principle of universal love and *sarvodaya* to fight for their liberation. Gandhi never distinguished between people on the basis of race or religion. He on the other hand always said that India was a place for the people of all races and all religions. "I do not except India of my dreams to develop one religion, i.e., to be wholly Hindu, or wholly Christian, or wholly Mussalman, but I want it to be wholly tolerant with all its religions working side by side with one another. Nobody had the right to take his race or religion as superior to others and rule over the latter on that plea. This was against the principle of *ahimsā* and *sarvodaya*."[81]

That Gandhi's concept of *swarāj* did not contravene his concept of *Sarvodaya*, will be clearer still if we see that even as his political goal Gandhi took not only *swarāj* but *purna-swarāj*, to be his real goal. *Purna-swarāj* was to be attained, according to Gandhi, not simply by the substitution of home rule for foreign rule. It was really achieved when it was for the welfare of all, and everyone felt his definite role in the government of the country. Moreover, under it, everyone could satisfy at least the minimum needs of his life. So real *swarāj* was only political freedom, but also economic freedom, and above all, freedom of the soul. Real *swarāj* was the *swarāj* of the poor and the neglected. "The *swarāj* of my dream is the poor man's *swarāj*. The necessities of life should be enjoyed by you in common with those enjoyed by the princes and the monied men. But that does not mean that you should have palaces like theirs. They are not necessary for happiness. You or I would be lost in them. But, you ought to get all the ordinary amenities of life that a rich man enjoys. I have not the slightest doubt that *swarāj* is not *purna-swarāj* until these amenities are guaranteed to you under it."[82]And again, "The swarāj of my dream recognises no race or religious distinction... *Swarāj* is to be for all... but emphatically including the maimed, the blind, the starving, toiling millions."[83] These lines clearly echo the same note which we have seen Gandhi sounding through his concept of *sarvodaya* and therefore it cannot be said that his concept of swarāj was in any way in conflict with his concept of *sarvodaya*.

At last, we should realize it clearly that political freedom of Gandhi was merely a prelude to the real freedom, the true *swarāj*. True *swarāj* consisted for him in every one's rule upon himself, such that all lower selfish motives were either removed or restrained and every man was related to all others by the thread of love. Even political *swarāj*, we have seen, could be won, according to Gandhi, by the path of complete love, self-suffering and self-sacrifice. And these were all the ways of the realization of *moksha*, or God or Truth. So real *swarāj* Gandhi took as synonymous with *moksha* itself.

References

1. *Harijan*, March 1936
2. *Young India*, December 1931, p. 428
3. *Yeravda Mandir*, Chap II
4. Introduction to *An Autobiography*, (1966), p. 11
5. *Young India*, July 1931
6. *Yeravda Mandir*, Vol III
7. *Ibid*
8. *Yeravda Mandir*, 1945
9. *Young India*, August 1920, p. 03
10. *Speeches and writings of Mahatma Gandhi*, IVth ed.
11. Raghavan N. Iyer,
12. V. K. Jhavari and D. G. Tendulkar (ed.) *Mahātma*, Vol-1951-54, p. 159
13. *Young India*, August 1920
14. *Ibid, April 1931*
15. *Ibid, June 1927*
16. *Ibid*, August 1920
17. *Ibid, June 1927*

18. *Harijan*, July 1940
19. *Ibid*
20. *Young India*, November, 1926
21. *Ibid*
22. *Harijan*, July 1940
23. *Young India*, November, 1925
24. *Ibid*, March 1931
25. *Ibid*, August 1929
26. A. Huxley, *Ends and Means*, (London, 1941) p. 52
27. *Young India*, July 1924, p. 236
28. *Yeravada Mandir*, 1945
29. *Young India*, June 1925, p. 191
30. M. K. Gandhi, *Truth is God*, (Ahmedabad, 1955), p. 139
31. *Harijan*, April 1946
32. A. Schweitzer, *Indian Thought and its Development* (1936) p. 231
33. *The Essential Gandhi*, p. 207.
34. *The Selected works of Mahatma Gandhi* (Ahmedabad, 1968), Vol. III, 150-51.
35. *Letter to Madama Privat*, Dec. 1947.
36. *The Selected Works*, Vol. VI, p. 183.
37. *Young India*, Aug. 1929.
38. *Ibid.* June, 1925.
39. Quoted by Raghavan Iyer in *op. cit.*, p. 287.
40. *Young India*, March 1921.
41. *Ibid.*
42. *Ethical Religion*, p. 45.
43. Chandrashekhar Shukla, *Conversations of Gandhijee*, p. 127.
44. *Ibid.*
45. *The Essential Gandhi*, pp. 209-10.
43. *Harijan*, April, 1939.
44. *Young India*, Dec., 1921.
45. *Ibid.*
46. *Young India.*
47. *The Selected Works*, Vol. VI, p. 200.
48. *Harijan*, June, 1936.
49. *Ibid.*

50. *Manu,* VI. 8.
51. *Manu,* VI. 3.
52. *Young India,* Dec. 1924.
53. *Young India,* Sept., 1924.
54. *Young India,* Dec. 1926.
55. *Selections from Gandhi,* p. 47.
56. *The Essential Gandhi,* p. 229.
57. *TheSpeeches and Writings of Mahatma Gandhi,* p. 301.
58. *Young India,* March 1922.
59. *Harijan,* Jan. 1937.
60. Jay Prakash Narayan, *Samajawada, Sarvodaya Aur Lokatantra* (Hindi), p. 172.
61. Ibid.
62. Paul Tillich, *Christianity and the Encounter of World Religions,* PP, 69-12.
63. *Young India,* March, 1931.
64. Ibid., Dec. 1920.
65. Ibid., June, 1924.
66. *All men are Brothers,* pp. 138-39.
67. *The Selected Works,* Vol. IV, p. 97.
68. *Speeches and Writings of Mahatma Gandhi* (Nateson 1934) (p. 409.
69. *Harijan,* March, 1939.
70. *Young India,* June, 1924.
71. Ibid., Feb. 1930.
72. Ibid., Jan. 1925.
73. Ibid., April, 1931.
74. Ibid., Nov. 1924.
75. *All men are Brothers,* p. 120.
76. *Yeravda Mandir,* p. 93.
77. *The Selected Works,* Vol. VI, p. 248.
78. *Young India,* Dec. 1927.
79. Ibid, March, 1931.
80. Ibid., Sept. 1925.

❑

Chapter-IV

Economic Concepts

(A) SWADESHI

The term '*swadeshi*' literally means belonging to or made in one's own country. Gandhi used the term for expressing or evoking one's love for the articles belonging to or made in one's own country. He wanted his countrymen to use as far as possible the articles produced or prepared in India and boycott those made somewhere else. And it was to symbolize this wish that he used the term '*swadeshi*'. By way of defining this term, Gandhi himself said, "The broad definition of *Swadeshi* is the use of all home-made articles to the exclusion of foreign things in so far as such use is necessary for the protection of home industries, more specially those industries without which India will become pauperized."[1] *Swadeshi*, therefore, so far looks to be mainly an economic concept and symbolizes Gandhi's sense of patriotism, i.e., his love for the articles made in his own country. But it meant many things more for him than merely the use of home-made articles. His *swadeshi* was a symbol of all-round exalted patriotism of a spiritual nature. He took it as a religious and spiritual discipline. According to him, the aim of *Swadeshi* was to enable the individual to realize his spiritual unity with all life. It was, according to him, engrained in the basic nature of man and stood for the final emancipation of the soul from the earthly bondage. All these things show that Gandhi's concept of *swadeshi* contained much more than what he looked ordinarily to convey through it. We will have to see here what that more could really be.

Swadeshi of Gandhi's conception broadly involved the idea that one had a natural moral obligation towards one's neighbour to the exclusion of those remotely situated. In Gandhi's own words "*Swadeshi* is that spirit in us which restricts us to the use of service of our immediate surroundings to the exclusion of the more remote."[2] Gandhi is generally regarded as a votary of universal love and service and therefore quite naturally it will be said that his doctrine of *swadeshi* in the above sense goes against that spirit of universal service. But it is not so, as Gandhi himself explained it. He took *swadeshi* as 'The acme of universal service'. Explaining the reason why he preached love and service of the neighbour in preference to those who were remotely situated, Gandhi said that our capacity for service was limited because we were all finite human beings. We could not serve all at the same time even if we so wanted. So we must as our first duty dedicate ourselves to the services of the nearest, our immediate neighbours. *Swadeshi* is thus based upon the recognition of the 'scientific limitation of the human capacity for service'. [3]But still it is an acme of universal service, because if the law of *swadeshi* is followed by everyone in strict dedication and sincerity, each one's service towards one's neighbour will naturally extend to become the service of all. Thus Gandhi laid down a condition with his doctrine of *swadeshi* that, "the neighbour thus served has in his turn to serve his own neighbour."[4] The service of sacrifice that each individual made for his neighbour would as a matter of logical consequence extend to the service of all. As Gandhi said ".... the logical conclusion of self-sacrifice was that the individual sacrificed himself for the community, the community sacrificed itself for the district, the district for the province, the province for the nation and the nation for the world."[5] Thus Gandhi's *swadeshi*, when properly understood, does not go against the spirit of *sarvodaya* and it is here that we can see that although his call for the national *swaraj* was prompted by his *swadeshi* spirit, still it was not a replica of his narrow nationalism. Just as the Christian teaching 'Love thy neighbour as thyself' is a symbol of universal love and service, similarly Gandhi's concept of *swadeshi* contains within it the germs of *savodava* and universal service.

Even in calling for the use of country-made goods to the exclusion of foreign goods, Gandhi was not really showing any hatred for the foreign goods, nor was he in any way propounding a doctrine of narrow nationalism. His intention must be quite clear from his view that the use of country-made goods was necessary only to that extent to which it was necessary to save our home industries. But to reject foreign goods simply because they were foreign was to make a fetish of *swadeshi* which Gandhi never liked. He regarded the production of such goods for which there was no suitable or congenial atmosphere in the country as a sheer waste of time and energy and he recommended the import of foreign goods in such condition. His own statement is very clear in this regard, "To reject foreign manufactures merely because they are foreign, and to go on wasting national time and money in the promotion in one's country of manufactures for which it is not suited would be criminal folly, and a negation of the swadeshi spirit."[6] Gandhi mainly emphasized the protection of such heavy industries and the use of *swadeshi* goods without which the country would be pauperized and the countrymen would be unemployed. Gandhi always thought of such industries as suitable for India which could give maximum employment to its toiling millions. He was of firm belief that "No scheme of irrigation or other agricultural improvement that human ingenuity can conceive can deal with the vastly scattered population of India or provide work for the masses of mankind who are constantly thrown out of employment."[7] And therefore he was of the opinion of installing a network of cottage industries in India instead of the big industries. In this connection he gave maximum importance to the spinning wheel *(Charkhā)* and the *Khādi*. He described *Charkhā* as "the symbol of non-violent economic self-sufficiency"[8] and *Khādi* as "the first indispensable step towards the discharge of *swadeshi* dharma towards society"[9] and also as a necessary and the most important corollary of the principle of *swadeshi*. Through *Charkhā* and *Khādi*, Gandhi actually wanted to give employment to the millions of his countrymen who were thrown out of employment. This emphasis on *Khādi* as an emblem of *swadeshi* adversely effected the cotton industry of Great Britain and many employees of the Lancashire textile industry were thrown out of employment. This apparently went contrary to Gandhi's *sarvodaya,* but Gandhi justified his action on the argument that his call for *swadeshi* and consequently for *Charkhā* or *Khādi* was not inspired by any hatred against anyone, rather it was inspired by his deep love for his countrymen, specially the millions poor. He was sorry that his call for *Khādi* had adversely affected the workers of Lancashire textile industry, but his immediate *dharma* towards his countrymen left no way out for him. Thus although theoretically, as Gandhi himself claimed, his *swadeshi* could be reconciled with his concept of *sarvodaya,* on practical levels the two might not always go together. For this, Gandhi would perhaps again advance the same solution that as human beings it was our duty to make our best efforts to realize our ideal, although our practical limitations might not always make us able to do so perfectly. That should not in any way deter us from pursuing our ideal and do the best possible in situations of moral dilemma. We have found Gandhi giving similar counsels in case of the pursuit of *ahimsā* also.

Thus apart from certain practical exceptions for which Gandhi always made room in his scheme of thought, *swadeshi* is not opposed to *sarvodaya.* Rather keeping in view the human limitations of the power of service, it is the best conceived means to *sarvodaya.* We have seen that the idea that one has a moral obligation towards his immediate neighbour does not exclude the idea that one has a duty towards all. Thus *swadeshi* and *sarvodaya* are not mutually exclusive concepts. They can rather both be regarded as the two different means to realize one's unity with all beings. *Swadeshi,* as Gandhi has said, is ingrained in human nature. It is *Gitā's swadharma* applied to one's immediate environment. Man by virtue of having a soul within him feels a natural affinity towards his fellow beings, because in the realm of soul he participates a common element with all others. Further deciphering the spiritual nature of his *swadeshi,* Gandhi went to the extent of saying that it stood for the final emancipation of the soul from all earthly bondage. On the face, it may seem that such statements mark merely the attempts of Gandhi to idealise his concepts. There was nothing very significant in them for any one to go deep into and try to understand. But if we analyse the concept of *swadeshi* and relate it to other concepts of

Gandhi in the context of his understanding of the concepts of man, God, *moksha* etc., we will see that there is a deep sense in the above statement of Gandhi and it is not just a result of irresponsible idealisation. According to Gandhi, *moksha* is self-knowledge which is the same as the knowledge or the realization of God or Truth. Now again, we have seen that Truth or God can be realized according to him only through the service of our fellow beings, specially the poor and the neglected. And it is this spirit of loving or spirit serving our fellow beings which is basically ingrained in the concept of *swadeshi*. *Swadeshi* is love for and service of one's fellowmen which, if truly followed, extends to the love of the people of the whole world. And it is only through such means that one's emancipation from worldly bondage can be affected. Thus *swadeshi* followed in its true spirit really stands for the final emancipation of man from the bondage of the world.

(B) BREAD LABOUR

Gandhi's concept of bread labour basically involves the idea that everybody should earn his bread by his own physical labour. Mere intellectual labour is not enough. Howsoever important work a man might be doing in terms of intellectual labour, that does not matter much unless he does some physical labour also to produce at least a part of his bread by himself. Gandhi here seems to be very much influenced by the Biblical sermon 'Earn thy bread by the sweat of the brow'. He has actually quoted this sermon in his own writings and has advised to follow the counsel in letter and spirit. The idea of bread labour first came to Gandhi by his study of Tolstoy, who in his turn seems to have got this idea from a Russian writer T. N. Bondaref. Gandhi was also influenced in this connection by the ideas expressed in Ruskin's *Unto This Last*. He also interprets *Gita's* theory of *yajna* or sacrifice in his own way and took it as a repository of the concept of bread labour. About the influences that made Gandhi form his concept of bread labour, he himself wrote as follows-"The law, that to live man must work, first came home to me upon reading Tolstoy's writing on Bread labour. But even before that I had begun to pay homage to it after reading Ruskin's *Unto*

This Last. The divine law, that man must earn his bread by labouring with his own hands, was first stressed by a Russian writer named T. M. Bondaref. Tolstoy advertised it and gave it wider publicity.

In my view, the principle has been set forth in the third chapter of the *Gitā*, where we are told that he who eats without offering sacrifice, eats stolen food. Sacrifice here can only mean Bread labour."[10] So, unless one labours with his own hands, he has no moral right to eat his food. This, according to Gandhi, is the sermon of the *Gitā* and the Bible alike. The *Gitā* doctrine of work depicted in the following verses was also interpreted by Gandhi as a doctrine of physical labour and taking help from them he said that those who did not perform physical labour were living a vain life and had no right to eat their bread :

> *Istānbhogānh ivo devā dāsyante yajñ ābhāvitah*
> *Tairdattānapradāyaibhy ayo bhunkte stena eva sah.*[11]
> *Evam pravartitm chakram nanuvartayatiha yah*
> *Aghayurindiyārāmo mogham pārtha sejivati.*[12]

Gandhi took Edwin Arnold's rendering of the verses in his *Song Celestial* to be the conveyers of the real meaning of them and these renderings run as follows :

> The gods will grant to Labour, when it pays
> Tithes in the altar-flame. But if one eats
> Fruits of the earth, rendering to kindly Heaven
> No gift of toil, that thief steals from his world.[13]
> He that abstains
> To help the rolling wheels of this great world,
> Glutting his idle sense, lives a lost life,
> Shameful and vain.[14]

So, he who abstains from physical work and does not pay to gods by the toil of his own labour lives a shameful and vain life. This was Gandhi's understanding of the verses and therefore he took them as endorsing his concept of bread labour.

Gandhi took agriculture to be the true symbol of bread labour, but he realized the fact that everybody could not take to agriculture. Therefore, he advised people to take up any kind of physical labour, such as, spinning, weaving, carpentry, scavenging, etc. However, with all considerations in view, Gandhi took spinning through *charkha* to be the fittest and most acceptable sacrificial body-labour. He said about this labour, "I cannot imagine anything nobler and more national than that for, say, one hour in the day we should all do the labour that the poor must do, and thus identity ourselves with them and through them with all mankind. I cannot imagine better worship of God than that in His name I should labour for the poor even as they do. The spinning wheel spells a more equitable distribution of the riches of the earth."[15] Thus Gandhi took *Charkhā* to be a symbol of equality and through that he sought the realization of the identity of all beings. In fact, through his concept of bread labour, Gandhi intended in to bring about a sense of equality amongst all men by causing them to realize the dignity of labour and consequently the dignity of man. He took this as a true and effective method of self-realization. Self-realization is God-realization, and God-realization is possible only when we identify ourselves with the lowest in the society. Bread labour, we have seen, effects that identity in a very significant and impressive manner. Thus, the importance of the concept of bread labour in Gandhian thought cannot be overemphasized. He wanted to affect a silent revolution in the structure of the society through it by bridging the gap between the rich and the poor, between the highly educated intellectuals and manual labourers. In fact, he wanted to obliterate all distinctions of rank through it. He himself said in this connection, "If all worked for their bread, distinctions of rank would be obliterated...."[16]Again deciphering the great potentials of the concept of bread labour, he said, "Obedience to the law of Bread labour will bring about a silent revolution in the structure of the society. Men's triumph will consist in substituting the struggle for existence by the struggle for mutual service. The law of the brute will be replaced by the law of man."[17]

(C) TRUSTEESHIP

Quite in accordance with his principle of the unity of mankind, Gandhi very much deplored the economic inequality prevalent specially amongst the people of India, Some were so rich that they had no legitimate use for their riches and again some were so poor that they could not have even one full meal every day. This Gandhi took as a real example of tyranny and injustice. He believed that there could be no economics devoid of morality and the latter demanded that the poor had as much right on the property of a nation as the rich had. It was a gross moral injustice that the rich lived so lavishly and the poor did not possess even that much which could satisfy their minimum needs. There must be an equal distribution of the wealth of the world amongst the rich and the poor alike. But Gandhi fully realized that perfectly equal distribution of the wealth of the world could only be an attractive ideal and never a practicable proposition.

He therefore preached equitable distribution. "My ideal is equal distribution, but so far as I can see, it is not to be realized. I therefore work for equitable distribution."[18] By 'equitable distribution' Gandhi meant such distribution which could give everybody at least that much wherewithal whereby he could satisfy his minimum needs. To each according to his needs was in short, the Gandhian principle of economic equality. Thus the economic equality of Gandhi's conception did not mean that everybody would literally have the same amount of wealth and economic goods. It simply meant that everybody should have enough for his or her needs. His concern of the poor and his conception of the economic equality of the rich and the poor can very well be seen through his following lines: "The contrast between the rich and the poor today is a painful sight. The poor villagers are exploited by the foreign government and also by their own countrymen—the city dwellers. They produce the food and go hungry. They produce milk and their children have to go without it. It is disgraceful. Everyone must have a balanced diet, a decent house to live in, facilities for the education of one's children and medical relief."[19] This constituted Gandhi's idea of economic equality.

And for this, i.e., for the economic equality of his conception, Gandhi appealed to the rich for real sacrifice. To impress upon the rich that keeping wealth disproportionate to their needs was virtually a kind of moral crime, he invoked the ancient Indian ideals of non-possession *(aparigraha)* and non-stealing *(asteya)* which constituted the essential parts of the cardinal virtues laid down in Hinduism, Jainism and Buddhism. Everything was God's, as depicted in the important first verse of the *Ishopanishad*, and therefore every one of us should have a spirit of complete detachment towards the riches of the world. As Gandhi said, "... everything belonged to God and was from God. Therefore it was for his people as a whole, not for a particular individual."[20] Thus Gandhi wanted to teach the lesson of *asteya* and *aparigraha* to the rich people so that they could have the wisdom, honesty and compassion enough for voluntarily sharing their riches with the poor and the needy. Gandhi firmly believed in the path of undefiled non-violence and therefore in spite of his clear realization that the rich were unjust enough to hoard a lot of wealth, he never wanted or advised to adopt the path of violence to snatch away their property and distribute it amongst the poor.

Gandhi, no doubt, liked the communistic ideal of economic equality, but he was totally averse to communism because of its sanction of the means of violence for securing economic equality. Gandhi feared that, "A violent and bloody revolution is a certainty one day unless there is voluntary abdication of riches."[21] He, therefore, fervently appealed to the rich people to share their riches voluntarily to avoid any future violence.

The name that Gandhi gave to this voluntary sharing of riches was Trusteeship. The essence of the doctrine of trusteeship, as Gandhi conceived it, is that a rich man be allowed to possess his property without being forcibly deprived of it, but he must have the honesty and good sense to spend a reasonable amount of his wealth to satisfy his own needs and then act as a trustee for the remainder of his property such that this remainder might be used for the benefit of the society as a whole. Gandhi appealed to the rich to exercise self-restraint on their part and reduce their needs to a minimum for the sake of the starving millions. Gandhi was not fundamentally opposed to luxurious life, but then he felt that unless the poor were able to satisfy even their minimum needs, it was a crime to go in for luxury. If the country was affluent enough to provide everybody for a luxuries life, it could well be led. But in the present conditions, the rich are required to exercise self-restraint and austerity. Gandhi advised the rich to relinquish the instinct of hoarding. He said that God had no need to store nor did he like that people should unnecessarily hoard. We must have faith in God and believe that he would arrange for our day-to-day needs. 'Take no thought for the morrow' was an injunction which according to Gandhi was contained in almost every religion of the world.

Further elaborating his concept of trusteeship, Gandhi pointed out that the ownership of the property would always vest in the individual himself, but he would hold his property voluntarily in trust, as if, it was the property of the society. He would increase the property by the use of his worth and talent, but always for the sake of the people. The State would regulate the rate of commission which he would get commensurate with the service rendered and its value to society. His children would also inherit the stewardship of the property, but only when they proved their fitness for it.

Gandhi's principle of trusteeship was ridiculed by many on the ground that it showed Gandhi's utter ignorance of man's natural instinct of acquisition and hoarding. It was said that Gandhi's so-called voluntary socialism proposed to be brought through the doctrine of trusteeship was simply a utopia which could never be realized. Nobody could be voluntarily ready to share his wealth with others. But Gandhi was firm to the last that his doctrine of trusteeship provided the only nonviolent means for bringing about economic equality. As equality brought about by force and violence could never be acceptable to him, he hoped that some day the rich could be converted to act as trustees of their property for the sake of the society. He however advised that if the rich did not listen to the pious words of voluntary sacrifice, such non-violent means as non-co-operation and civil disobedience could be used against them. Gandhi firmly asserted that there could be no accumulation of wealth and capital without the help and co-operation of the workers. If they withdrew their co-operation and adopted the path of non-violent civil disobedience, the rich and the capitalists would have to realize their mistakes and they would be ready to give due share to the poor workers. Gandhi however never endorsed the use of violent means to coerce the capitalists to relinquish their wealth. He had firm faith in the inner goodness of man. He distinguished between capitalism and capitalists and asserted that only the former was to be removed., not the latter. We must remember his lines here that

".... no human being is so bad as to be beyond redemption, no human being is so perfect as to warrant his destroying him whom he wrongly considers to be wholly evil."[22]Gandhi wanted to bring social revolution by change of heart and not by violence and coercion. And that he thought was possible by sincerely following the paths of *ahimsā* and *satyāgraha*. Gandhi was never in favour of destroying the capitalists because according to him 'destruction of the capitalist must mean destruction, in the end, of the worker'.[23] and also because it will be like 'killing the hen that lays golden eggs'.[24] Here it may be argued that even adopting the path of non-cooperation and civil disobedience against the capitalists amounts to a kind of coercion. But this is the same old question which we have already discussed in our chapter on *Satyāgraha* and therefore we would not like here to go once again into the details of the answer to the objection.

References

1. *Speeches and Writings etc.* p. 275.
2. *Harijan*, March, 1947.
3. *Ibid.*
4. *Speeches and Writings*, etc. p. 281.
5. *Yeravda Mandir*, pp. 96-97.
6. *Young India*, Nov. 1921.
7. *The Selected Works*, Vol. VI, p. 293.
8. *Young India*, June, 1931.
9. *Ibid.*
10. *Yeravda Mandir*, p. 50.
11. *Gitā*, III. 12.
12. *Ibid,* Ill. 16.
13. *Selections from Gandhi*, p. 50.
14. *Ibid.*
15. *Young India*, Oct., 1921.
16. *Yeravda Mandir*, p. 50.
17. *Harijan,* June, 1935.
18. *Young India*, March, 1927.

19. *Harijan*, March, 1946.
20. *Ibid.* Feb. 1947.
21. *Selections from Gandhi*, p. 77.
22. *Young India*, March, 1931.
23. *Ibid.*
24. *Ibid.*

❑

Chapter-V

Assessment and Conclusion

We have made an attempt in our foregoing pages to see the impact of the different religions on the formation of some of the more important Gandhian concepts. Even a not very careful reader of these pages cannot perhaps fail to mark that the impact of Hinduism has been the greatest upon Gandhi. C. F. Andrews seems to be perfectly right when he remarks, "The more we study Mahatma Gandhi's own life and teaching, the more certain it becomes that the Hindu religion has been the greatest of all influences in shaping his ideas and actions."[1] He has formulated his concepts under the primary impact of Hinduism, although he has found substantial support for his. views in many religions of the world other than Hinduism also. For all practical purposes Gandhi did not deem Jainism and Buddhism as religions separate from Hinduism and therefore a formidable impact of these religions also can be seen on him unfailingly. But, as we have seen, he was not less impressed by some of the ideas present in Christianity and Islam also and on many points these religions had decisive effect upon him. In any case, our previous pages are definite pointers to the fact that fundamentally Gandhi was convinced to the inner depth of his heart about some of the metaphysical truths regarding the nature of God and man and all the rest of his ideas or concepts were in some sense or other the necessary consequences of these convictions. He believed in advaita and in his own way of presenting it, he said that, as God was all-pervasive *Sat*, nothing really existed beyond and besides God. In every man and in the entire creation, the same *Sat* was present and therefore there was a basic unity behind the seeming multiplicity. Everything was God's and everything was in God. Gandhi thus firmly believed in the unity of the entire existence. Human soul is the spark of the Divine within man and thus in that respect all men are one. Moreover, all men are inherently divine in nature. There can therefore be no distinction of higher and lower between man and man. With the Jains, Gandhi believed that every individual of the human or subhuman level possessed a soul, dormantly or fully conscious, and therefore on the inner level the entire creation was one. In all these, Gandhi brought about a splendid blending between the Hindu advaitism and the Jaina relativism. Generally, Vedantic advaitism and Jaina pluralism and relativism are taken as theories poles apart, but Gandhi tried to reconcile them in his own way and we can well see that he has maintained this spirit of reconciliation in all the spheres of his thought and action. God, as all-pervasive *Sat,* is absolute, but we are able to know him only relatively. In other words, Truth is absolute but our knowledge of it is only partial and relative. *Ahimsā* as a moral virtue is absolute, but its practice may be relative to the specific circumstances. *Satyāgraha* as a mode of life is absolute, but its practice may seek compromises on special occasions or in specific situations. *Sarvodaya* is the absolute ideal, but its attainment may be only partial and relative. In all, Gandhi recognised the absolute nature of Truth, but he at the same time also recognised the limitations of human knowledge and capacity. Universal love (and service) was his ideal, but the relative fulfilment of that he visualised through *swadeshi.* He wanted every man to accept certain moral values as absolute and try to realize them in his life to the best of his capacity, but he always allowed legitimate concessions because he knew that man was after all man having limited capacities.

Gandhi did a great job in reconciling spiritualism with social service, religion with morality. Of course, he was not alone in this. Modern Indian thinkers like Vivekanand and Tagore also accompanied him in doing the same sort of job. But Gandhi's speciality lies in the fact that he did not bring about the reconciliation only in theory, rather he gave it a concrete shape by practising it in actual life also. He always devoted himself to the acts of social service and believed that through this kind of service he was actually realising his real self or God. Gandhi said that he believed in *advaita* but *advaita* in Indian tradition had got a very mystical sort of meaning, according to which *Brahman* alone was the reality and all else a mere dream or illusion. Man's true goal was to realize *Brahman* and for that the path of *nivrtti* was essential. Some sort of *sadhana* or meditation was necessary and for that one had to renounce the world. But Gandhi brought the philosophy of *Advaita* on a very practical level and interpreted its metaphysics in somewhat a practical and ethical manner. *Advaita* implied for him that the basic Truth was only one and the entire creation was the expression of the same Truth. There was no difference, therefore, between one being and another. All were basically one. There was an identity between God and self and there was a basic unity in the entire existence. *Moksha* or salvation, therefore, did not require one to go to the jungle by renouncing the world for *sādhanā* or meditation. The best *sādhanā* was to love the entire creation. It is in and through love that God or self could be realized. So, *Brahma* or God realization was nothing else than the realization of the basic unity underlying all existence and that could be done only by realizing oneself into others and others into oneself. This again could be done by sincere love for all beings, i.e., by the adoption of the path of true *ahimsā*. Working for *sarvodaya* was therefore working for the attainment of *moksha* or the realization of God. The social and the spiritual goals were not different. They were basically one and the same. In the true spirit of the *Gitā*, Gandhi taught not the renunciation of the world but renunciation in the world. It is only by a selfless service of others that one could realize God or *Brahman*. There was no other way out. What was necessary for *moksha* was not the giving up of the world, but the giving up of selfish motives. There was nothing like narrow egoistic self. All selves were bound in an essential bond of unity and therefore egoism was a blatant illusion. Social service and love towards all were the only means of self-realization, God-realization or *Moksha*, whatever that might be called.

Quite in line with his above views Gandhi redefined religion in his own way. He took religion not as something which the individual does with (or in) his solitariness, but as that which he does amongst his fellow beings. According to him religion is a way of life and therefore it consists in the activities of every moment that one does in his daily life and not in certain special actions that he does at certain special moments. Religion is life-orientation and such a life-orientation for Gandhi consists mainly in a life of love, sacrifice and suffering. Of course, a way of life is not rootless. It has a firm foundation in some kind of vision, some kind of inner experience. That may be taken as the mystical side of religion, and with respect to that aspect religion is in a sense individualistic too. Gandhi here quite in tune with the great Indian scholar Dr Radhakrishnan seems to believe that vision and action, mysticism and ethics go together.[2] There can thus be no hard and fast distinction between religion and morality. In the vision, we have a glimpse of the Reality or Truth which is absolute but this glimpse by itself is always relative. The vision of one man therefore will naturally differ from the other. All the great religions of the world are the results of the original vision of some or other prophet or saint like the Buddha, Mohammad or Jesus Christ. But any one's vision of Truth can only be relative. Hence all the religions of the world are relatively true, all of them express the same absolute Truth in their own relative ways. All are therefore imperfect in one sense and true in another sense. None can claim superiority over the other. Religious tolerance, therefore, is a necessity. We must have respect and regard for each other's religion, because everyone's religion reveals to him the nature of the absolute Truth in his own relative and partial way. The basic truth behind all the religions, however, is one and therefore there is an underlying unity between them. Quarrel in the name of religion has thus got no meaning. Also, conversions from one religion to another by the use of force or material inducements are immoral and undesirable. Gandhi much criticized the working of the Christian missionaries on this point because they were engaged converting poor Hindus to Christianity by offering material inducements to them. Gandhi totally decried such a business of religion in the false name of charity. We have also seen him criticizing the false Christian claim that Jesus is the only begotten son of God. He said that all prophets of all religions were equally great, and no special status could be given to any one of them. Claiming superiority for one's own religion over others was very wrong and misleading, according to Gandhi, and such tendencies must be given up. However, he never decried voluntary conversions. If one felt that he would get greater spiritual satisfaction by adopting some other religion, he was free to do so and nobody had the right to check him or criticize him. There was no need of any Universal or World Religion. What was needed was a true sense of tolerance towards other religions which meant love and respect for them, because all religions at bottom spoke of the same Truth.

Gandhi also did a great job in emphasizing, perhaps for the first time in modern Indian thought, upon the purity of means as a necessary condition for the attainment of a good end. In this also Gandhi's deep sense of respect and regard for the moral and religious way of life was speaking from within him. Apart from a moral and religious way of life in which *ahimsā* or love had to play the most prominent role, no desirable end could be achieved. Gandhi was so convinced about the necessity of the purity of means by his study of religions like Jainism, Buddhism and Christianity, that even for the attainment of such ends for which the path of violence was necessary in the eyes of people, he practised the path of non-violence, *satyāgraha* and self-suffering and achieved dazzling results out of them. By introducing religion into politics, he wanted to achieve rarest political goals through the means of *ahimsā* or love and his immediate political goal, the *swarāj*, was really attained by him through such means. Gandhi was sometimes criticized by such great thinkers as Tilak and Tagore. These thinkers called him a puritan, a religious fanatic, who unnecessarily impeded the path of the freedom of India by teaching ascetic values which had got absolutely no relevance in this sphere. With such an idea in mind, Tilak once wrote to Gandhi, "Politics is a game of worldly people, and not of *sadhus*, and instead of the maxim '*akkhodhenaji-nekkhodham*' (conquer anger by non-anger) as preached by Buddha, I prefer to rely on the maxim of Sri Krishna '*ye yatha mām parapadyante tamsthathiva bhaimyaham*' (In whatever way men resort to me, even so do I render to them)...... Both methods are equally honest and righteous but the one is more suited to this world than the other." In reply to this, Gandhi wrote, "For me there is no conflict between the two texts..... The Buddhist text lays down an eternal principle. The text from the *Bhagvat Gitā* shows to me how the principle of conquering hate by love, untruth by truth, can and must be applied. If it be true that God metes out the same measure to us that we mete out to others, it follows that if we would escape condign punishment, we may not return anger for anger but gentleness even against anger. And this is the law not for the unworldly but for the worldly. With deference to the *Lokamānya*, I venture to say that it betrays mental laziness to think that the world is not for *sadhus*. The epitome of religions is to promote *Purushārtha*, and *Pusushārtha* is nothing but a desperate attempt to become a *Sādhu* i.e., to become a gentleman in every sense of the term."[3] The ideas expressed here are neither very systematic nor very clear, but one thing seems quite obvious and that is that, Gandhi did not believe like Tilak that saintly virtues had a different sphere of application and that in the political sphere such virtues were not required. Gandhi could never be convinced that in politics even foul means, such as those of violence, hatred etc., could be employed to achieve the goal. Saintly virtues were as much applicable in the worldly sphere as in any other sphere. About the greatness, purity and efficacy of good means, Gandhi was so much convinced that he was not ready to make any compromise over it in any situation. He, in the perfect spirit of the *Gitā*, believed that we as human beings had our control only on the means and never on the end. The end was beyond our control. So, we should make every effort for maintaining the purity of means. Gandhi did not believe in the doctrine that means was after all means. For him means was after all everything. One could never achieve a pious goal by adopting a foul means. As he said, 'we could not expect a rose by planting a noxious weed'.

But despite these great contributions that Gandhi made to Indian thought and practice (as a matter of fact, to the world-thought and ways of practical behaviour) in the light of his deep religious convictions formed out of his essentially Hindu background as well as out of his serious studies of different world religions, Gandhi has so often been much criticized on various points. He has been termed as a day-dreamer, a utopian and a religious fanatic. His conception of man, for example, is so often cited and it is pointed out that he has unduly presented a very optimistic picture of man and has ignored his essentially animal or brute nature. Gandhi looked to common man quite unrealistically and presented an unnecessarily inflated picture of him. In himself, Gandhi might be a saint, a God-man, a pure divine soul, but it was unrealistic and utopian to impose his own image upon everyone. Every one can' t be a saint. Men are essentially of evil nature and they are disposed to all sorts of evil designs. But we may well see that Gandhi cannot be criticized in this way for his conception of human nature. We may very well remember that he never ignored the animal aspect of man, rather he fully recognised it and also realized that man was very often very easily prone to falling a victim to his animal drives. But then what he took to be the essential nature of man was certainly something far removed from this animal side. In his essential nature, man is spiritual and divine, because he contains as the inner and essential core of his being a soul which is really the divine spark within him. Man's soul is identical in nature with God according to Gandhi. In all these, Gandhi was depicting his essentially Hindu faith regarding the nature of man and God. He was, of course, influenced in this connection by the Jain belief also that every man had a soul and that the soul was capable of attaining divine hood by attaining the four infinite qualities of bliss, power, knowledge and faith *(anantachatusthaya)*. Gandhi believed that in general man was of course guided by his animal drives, but in his inner nature he was different. Even the most brutal of man could be converted into a man of saintly nature, if we could be able to arouse his spirit from within him. We have seen that it is on such a conception of nature of man that Gandhi built up his conception of *ahimsā* and *satyāgraha*, experimented throughout his social and political life with them and attained tremendous success. If Gandhi did not believe in the essential divinity of man, he could never have thought of winning over evil by good and hatred by love. Thus, his concept of man is fully consistent with his concept of *ahimsā* and *satyāgraha*. The conviction that self-suffering would definitely yield result could hold root in Gandhi only because he believed in the essential goodness of man. In his concept of man, Gandhi gave a secure metaphysical foundation to what Buddhism and Christianity took as a mere moral principle. So Gandhi's greatness does not so much lie in his formation of the concept of man as in his consistent application of his concept to the most challenging and complicated aspects of practical life, in which he also attained marvellous success. His concept of man was based on his essentially Hindu faith and therefore he cannot be blamed or criticized for that. One may very well have a different concept of man for himself. Conceptions regarding fundamental metaphysical truths like God, world and man are to a very great extent, matters of inner conviction and people might very well differ with regard to them. Nobody can claim a-priori that his concept of man is the best or the most authentic. The real test of the truth or validity of any concept is its successful and consistent practical application which Gandhi so truthfully and ably made.

Similarly, with regard to Gandhi's concept of *ahimsā*, it may be pointed out that it appears to be so comprehensive and demanding that it is really very difficult to practise it in life, specially in a political life. The same may be said with regard to *satyāgraha* also. It demands such an attitude on the part of man (which Gandhi has amply characterised as reducing oneself to Zero) that it is almost impossible for a man of ordinary qualities to qualify for it. Their observance requires saintly virtues which are characteristic of a man who has renounced everything and is completely devoid of fear and self-interest. Gandhi really said himself also that complete renouncing of fear and self-interest was necessary for the observance of true *ahimsā* or *satyāgraha*. But can everybody be a saint? These are therefore impracticable virtues. But such criticisms against Gandhi also are not completely in order. First of all, Gandhi did not only theorise about these virtues, rather he presented a complete example of the observance of them in his own practical life. Moreover, he himself conceded that although these virtues were to be taken as absolute and it was the duty of every one to practise them in maximum possible situations, but "life was not a single straight line" and it might be sometimes very difficult or even impossible to practise them literally. In such circumstances Gandhi allowed exceptions by fully realizing the limitations of human capacity. Gandhi himself talked of 'Euclidean' models and said that such models were not fully realizable in actual life. *Satya, ahimsā, satyāgraha* etc. were all taken by him as Euclidean models in their absolute nature, which were not perfectly realizable, but our duty was to make the sincerest efforts to realize these ideals as far as possible. We have found Gandhi making a useful distinction between absolute and relative truth. He has characterized Truth in its fundamental and inherent nature to be absolute, but man according to him is capable of realizing Truth only relatively and partially. The same applies to man's pursuit of the values of *ahimsā* and *satyāgraha* also. Gandhi took ethical values to be absolute, but still instead of preaching an absolutistic ethics, he preached a relativistic one in which man had the freedom to make suitable compromises with reference to specific situations of life.

Gandhi's concepts of *ahimsā* and *satyāgraha* are criticized on a different level also. Gandhi believed in change (whether social, political or economic) through persuasion and not through co-ercion and it is chiefly with this end in view that he propounded the doctrines of *ahimsā* and s*atyāgraha* as appropriate means. But it is pointed out that *ahimsā* and *satyāgraha* also, at bottom, are means of coercion and not of persuasion. Through self-suffering, the votary of *ahimsā* or *satyāgraha* really coerces the opponent for his demand to be conceded. The practical ways of *satyāgraha* that Gandhi usually recommended in the forms of non-cooperation, civil disobedience and fasting are all means of veiled coercion. But we have already seen in the chapters relating to *ahimsā* and *saryāgraha* that Gandhi has successfully disowned such charges of coercion to be levelled against his principles of *ahimsā* and *satyāgraha* and we need not repeat them here again.

We have seen above more than once that Gandhi made a distinction between absolute and relative truth. But it is so often pointed out against this distinction that in practice people may often take advantage of it for sticking to their own false beliefs or prejudices in the name of relative truths. If no man can ever attain absolute truth and what man is able to grasp is only relative truth, then the truths claimed to be achieved by different people may always remain in conflict with each other and no authentic or guaranteed claim about truth can ever be made. Such objections have been raised against Jaina relativism also. But if we try to see Gandhi's view in the context of his entire thought, we may find that he has been fully alive to the above kind of possibility and has laid down certain rigorous qualifying conditions for a man who claims to have a glimpse of Truth. Of course, Gandhi never compromised with his view that Truth was not the exclusive property of anyone, but then he did not take the realization of Truth such a petty matter that everybody could claim for his any and every opinion that it was a result of his own realization of Truth. We remember that to the question, 'What is Truth', Gandhi replied that it was what the voice within (i.e., conscience) told us. But again, he pointed out that before one made such claims of knowing Truth on the strength of inner voice, he must have fully disciplined himself by cultivating the virtues of truthfulness, humility, purity etc. and above all non-violence. He must also embrace the ideals of poverty and non-possession and must be completely free from ideas of self-interest. He pointed out that to tread the path of Truth was not an easy task. It was like moving on the edge of a sword; it was a *tapasyā*. Thus, although Truth was not the exclusive property of anyone, and everyone was capable of attaining to partial or relative truth, the man who claimed to attain to such truth must be a man of special moral qualities.

Criticisms are also levelled against Gandhi with regard to his concepts of *sarvodaya* and stateless democracy. It is pointed out that these are only examples of Gandhi's utopian ideas which could never be realized in actual practice. But without going into the details of these criticisms, we can summarily dispose them of here by reminding the critics of the repeated assertion of Gandhi that these were merely ideals with reference to which Gandhi wanted himself and others to work.

Ideals are not there always to be literally and perfectly achieved. They are rather the targets which regulate our activities from above and for which we always strive. Gandhi's famous saying that one step ahead was enough for him tells us amply of his real intention, aim and purpose behind fixing high targets and ideals. He was not a visionary or a utopian. He was rather a practical idealist, as he himself said. He fixed high targets before him in accordance with his fundamental metaphysical and religious beliefs and worked for his whole life in the light of them. What mattered for him was not that he achieved the ideal but that he moved a few steps ahead towards it. Gandhi's ideal of *sarvodaya* was fully in keeping with his conception of the equality of all beings and his ideal of stateless democracy was a logical sequel to his conception of the dignity of individual man. He had grave apprehensions about the evil designs of the power vested in the State and therefore to save the dignity of the individual man, he preached the ideal of stateless democracy.

Gandhi's economic concepts of *swadeshi* and bread labour have also been criticized. About *swadeshi*, as we have already seen, it has been pointed out that it is a symbol of narrow nationalism which does not fit in with Gandhi's conception of the equality of all men irrespective of caste, creed or nation. But it can be seen very well, as we have pointed out earlier also, that Gandhi's concept of *swadeshi* understood in its true perspective, does not in the least go against inter-nationalism, philanthropy and broad-based humanitarianism. It is only on the face that the doctrine of *swadeshi* seems to promote narrow nationalism. His concept of bread-labour has been ridiculed on the ground of its impracticability. It is said (or may be said) that Gandhi was by nature a utopian and talked of only such thing the practice of which was either impossible or unnecessary or rather harmful and retarding. What could be the wisdom of counselling even those who were engaged in high intellectual pursuits to undertake physical labour? Could they find enough time to do that much of physical labour which would produce their daily food? It may also be pointed out here that Gandhi unnecessarily dragged the scriptures to support his utopian ideas. To suit his purpose, Gandhi quite artificially interpreted the word 'work' *(Karma)* in the various verses of the *Bhagvad-Gita* to mean physical labour, By counselling to take the path of *karma*, *Gita* does not necessarily counsel to undertake the path of physical labour.' Work simply means here the path of *pravrtti* in place of the path of *nivrtti*, i.e., the path of the renunciation of the world to lead the life of a recluse. But such critics of Gandhi fail to realize the true nature of the ideal that Gandhi wanted to pursue by his concept of bread-labour. Gandhi was deeply concerned about the quality of life of the ordinary man who was engaged in physical labour. He wanted to give such a man the dignity that he truly deserved. Such men were really treated as low in the society only because they had to do hard physical labour. Those who were engaged in intellectual labour ruled over them and enjoyed a higher status. Gandhi, due to his deep faith in the equality of all men, could not tolerate this. And it is with a view to make the people of so-called higher status feel a sense of identity with the workers and labourers that he counselled them to undertake some sort of physical labour to earn their food. His bringing in of the *Gitā* philosophy of action (work) to substantiate his doctrine of bread-labour may or may not be correct, but his real intention behind his concept of bread-labour is quite clear. It was just to uphold the dignity of manual labour and to make the high-ups feel their basic unity with the lowest of human beings that he brought in this concept. The same concern for the dignity and quality of life of the ordinary worker may be seen in Gandhi's advocacy for *khadi* and such other small-scale industries in opposition to heavy industries. He believed that the economics of heavy industries had no place for the dignity and value of man. Man becomes the slave of his own creation. In the economics of heavy industrialization, what matters is capital. In place of it Gandhi wanted an economics in which people mattered. In more recent times, E. F. Schumacher has amply supported this Gandhian view of economics in his book *Small is Beautiful*. The sub-title of this book 'Economics as if people matter' is significant. This is what exactly Gandhi wanted to achieve through his opposition to big industries and his preference for *charkha* and *khadi*. His faith in the greatness of individual man, which has taken root in him through his studies of religions like Hinduism and Jainism, was really unshakable and in every thought that he put forward, whether social, political or economic, an echo of that faith can very well be heard.

We have referred earlier about Gandhi being branded a religious fanatic, who wanted to introduce religion everywhere, and saw in the fabric of his each and every concept an emblem of *moksha*. This was seen with an eye of scorn by all those who took them to be radicals, up-to-date and practical. By the introduction of religion into politics, it is said, Gandhi helped politicians of petty interests in the exploitation of religious emotions of people. One such example can be seen in Jinnah, who lived for the creation of a Muslim State, by exploiting Islamic sentiments of the Muslim population of India. Moreover, as Raghavan Iyer notes, introduction of religion into politics generally has a tendency to give rise to some kind of authoritarianism. Democratic attitudes prevail only there where religion is allowed to play no role in politics. But such misgivings are the results of misusing Gandhi's pious call for the introduction of religion into politics. He never meant by religion any particular religion and we have seen what a broad conception of religion he really had for himself. By the introduction of religion into politics he simply meant to found politics on a pure moral ground. Politics, as generally understood, is a nasty game of foul play where the purity of means is no body's concern. The only aim is the possession of power which could be achieved by any means. Gandhi, like a true saint, really wanted to eradicate this game of nasty and foul means from politics and wanted to find it on a pure moral ground. If people misused his call for the introduction of religion into politics by evoking religious sentiments of people for their petty aims, it was no fault of Gandhi. The fear of authoritarianism may also find support by such misuses of the pious name of religion. Some people may, by taking them to be the custodians of religion, misdirect people and dupe them to accept their own authority, but that again would be a nasty distortion of Gandhi's real intention behind introducing religion into politics. By introducing religion into politics, Gandhi never meant to give certain religious leaders authoritarian political roles in society. His intention was quite clear and he cannot be blamed for the misuse of his pious counsels of making politics pure and spiritual. If his views are taken in the right perspective, they are sure to foster a true sense of democracy based on *ahimsā* and Truth.

So far as the question of the idealization of his concepts is concerned, it is a fact that even in his seemingly political, economic and social concepts, Gandhi saw an emblem of the concept of *moksha* and to some it may look odd, farfetched, unnecessary and dogmatically traditional. But if one looks to Gandhi's views in the framework of his entire philosophical outlook, which will certainly include his views about God, man and other worldly beings, he will not find anything odd or unnecessary in Gandhi's thought. The concepts of *swadeshi* and *swaraj* certainly look to be purely economic and political concepts on the surface, but a careful reader will not fail to see that Gandhi never took these concepts as purely economic or purely political. In fact, as we have seen, there could be no politics without religion and no economics without moral or human basis for Gandhi. Therefore, there could be no purely political or purely economic concept in the Gandhian way of thinking. Gandhi took '*swadeshi*' no doubt in the sense of the use of country-made goods to the exclusion of foreign made goods, and to this extent it remains a purely economic concept. But going into the full details of Gandhi's understanding of the concept of *swadeshi* will reveal that it was only a part, and rather a superficial aspect of the meaning of the term '*swadeshi*' for Gandhi. In its deeper meaning it was, as he said, an "acme of universal service" for him and implied within it the ideals of universal love and brotherhood. So, in this sense, there was nothing unnatural in Gandhi's bringing his concept of *swadeshi* very near to the concept of *moksha* or self-realization. Self-realization was for Gandhi the realization of the absolute oneness of all beings at bottom. And the ideal of self-realization was to be achieved by following the path of universal love and brotherhood, which is a natural consequence of the doctrine of *swadeshi*. Similarly, *swaraj* as ordinary people understood it, meant nothing more than the removal of the British from India and bringing in self-rule over the country, but for Gandhi it never meant merely this. He clearly and openly said from the very start that self-rule for him never meant merely rule by the self, but also rule over the self. It meant self-restraint and self-purification. And if this is what he meant by *swarāj* it is quite natural that *swarāj* could not be taken to signify a mere political goal, it must have something very spiritual and religious in its inner depth of meaning and significance. A similar dismay is visible amongst people in the first instance when Gandhi's concept of *sarvodaya* is equated with the concept of *moksha* or self-realization, but, as we have seen in their deeper analysis, the two concepts really come very close and the curtain between the social and the spiritual begins to give way. In fact, the whole of Gandhi's life and thinking, as he has himself said, (see Introduction) were directed towards the ideal of *moksha* or self-realization and therefore there is no wonder if he has sought to fill in a content relating to *moksha* in each one of his concepts, whether social, political or economic. Even at the cost of repetition we will like to quote here his following lines once again, "Man's ultimate aim is the realization of God, and all his activities, social, religious have to be guided by the ultimate aim of the vision of God. The immediate service of all human beings becomes a necessary part of the endeavour, simply because the only way to find God is to see Him in His creation and be one with it. This can only be done by service of all."[4]

We have thus seen how through out his thought and practice, Gandhi has been a thoroughly religious man and all his important concepts have been formed under the impact of his deep religious conviction. His religious conviction and his concept of religion were basically formed under the ideas drawn from Hinduism, but he has no less been influenced in his thought by the essential elements of other religions of the world such as Buddhism, Jainism, Christianity and Islam. In fact, Buddhism and Jainism he never took as practically different from Hinduism and an echo of the essential elements of these religions can be marked everywhere in his thought. He also loved Christianity and Islam in their original, unadulterated forms and these also, specially Christianity, had certain turning effects on his thought. His ideas have, of course, been criticized, as we have seen, mostly on the ground that he has been very much utopian in his thought and has unnecessarily allowed religion to intrude everywhere. But such criticisms, as we have noted, are mostly unwarranted and cannot be validly levelled against Gandhi. To call him a utopian is a sheer misuse of the word, because whatever he has said, he has tried to translate into action too and his whole life has been a life of experiments with the ideals that he so strongly cherished and professed. His introduction of religion into politics and other such spheres may not look wise and desirable to those who take them to be ultra-moderns and who only like to accomplish results by whatever means that may become possible. But those who want real peace and progress in the world and who adduce utmost value to the dignity of individual man will ever appreciate Gandhi's deeply religious and moral outlook and his undaunted and unabated sense of suffering for the sake of humanity. What, after all, have we gained by seeking to keep religion and politics apart and by guarding against the intrusion of spiritual values in the social, political and economic spheres? What is the use of having big industries and the so-called great progress made by their help, if we have lost our peace of mind and real sense of ease and security? What, if we gain everything of the world, but lose our own soul? Petty sectarianism must be guarded against, as Gandhi himself repeatedly reminded us about, but true religion and morality have their due place in every sphere of human life. It is these which will bring real peace and progress of man. Gandhi may be branded as out-dated, backward, traditional and unprogressive in his outlook, but he has taught a great lesson to modern man, which if properly understood and thought over, will bring real peace and progress for him. Gandhi has played once again, in recent times, the role that was played by the *Upanishads* in India and Socrates in Greece in ancient times and by the Danish thinker Kierkegaard in modern times. The *Upanishads* took the knowledge of the self (*Ātmanāmviddhih*) to be the highest human ideal and both Socrates and Kierkegaard in their own ways raised and propagated the slogan 'know thyself' for man. The *Upanishads* relate that when *Yajnavalkya* left all his property to his wife *Maitreyi* and himself began to start for the jungle to lead a life of the recluse, *Maitreyi* asked, "What shall I do with all these things? Would these help me in gaining my soul?"[5]Similarly, Kierkegaard has exhorted people in modern times not to be mad after objective and scientific knowledge. He has asked them to return to their inward life and know their inner being. In the same spirit, Gandhi took it all useless to have big power structures and heavy industries, if man could not remain man. Gandhi had a very high image of man in his mind, as we have already seen, and he had a real concern for man to be man in the true sense of the term. If his conception of man is understood in its real spirit and everyone in the present world realizes the dignity of the individual man, all acts of suppression, tyranny, discrimination, apartheid etc. will automatically go away. Similarly, if one understands the real spirit of his philosophy of *advaita*, the rivalries between man and man, between one society and the other, between nation and nation will automatically vanish. If Gandhi was ever needed most, it is in the modern world in which people in spite of their great scientific and material achievements have not been able to achieve real peace of mind and all sorts of dissensions, bickering, mutual fears and cold wars are prevalent all over the universe. Critics have made a fun of Gandhi's idea of the introduction of religion into politics, but if religion in his sense is really introduced into national and international politics today and politics instead of remaining a game of foul play becomes morality based, every citizen of the world, who is leading a life of utmost tension and fear today, will begin to live a life of real peace and equanimity. In ancient India even battles were fought in accordance with moral principles. We have the concept of *dharma-yuddah* here. Because politics is absolutely devoid of morality today, there is everywhere an atmosphere of mutual distrust and doubt and people have lost their peace of mind. We can every well realize the relevance and value of the great teachings of Mahatma Gandhi today, if we honestly diagnose the state of our life that we are leading today. A great many of the quarrels on the national level and wars and fights on the international level, which have made the life of a great majority of people miserable, are due to the religious differences between people. People belonging to one religion take people of other religions as their enemies. In this context, the only remedy to save people is to bring in faithfully the lesson of religious tolerance and secularism as taught by Mahatma Gandhi. He clearly saw a unity amongst the religions of the world underlying their outward differences in forms and doctrines. He preached equal love and regard for all religions, because all of them depicted the same truth in their own ways. It was a sheer madness to quarrel in the name of religion, according to him. Religion was there to bind people together and not to dissect them into different groups and sects. By birth, Gandhi was a Hindu, but he blended the characteristics of various religions in such a manner in his character and personality that people generally confused whether he was a Hindu, or a Jain, or a Buddhist or a Christian or a 'Christian Mohammedan,' as it was sometimes called. As a matter of fact, he was all these at the same time and even more. [6] The world needs him most fervently today, if it has needed him ever at all.

References

1. C. F. Andrews, *Mahatma Gandhi's Ideas* (Allen & Unwin, 1949), p. 60.
2. S. Radhakrishnan, *Eastern Religions & Western Thought*, P. 80
3. *Young India*, Jan. 1920.
4. *Harijan*, Aug., 1936.
5. *Brh. up.* 2. 4. 1-3.
6. See B. R. Nanda, *Mahatma Gandhi, A Biography*, p. 11.

❏

Bibliography

A. Works on and by Gandhi

- M.K. Gandhi, *An Autobiography* (or *The story of My Experiments with Truth*), (Beacan Press, Boston, 1966 & Navajivan, Ahmedabad, 1956).

- M.K. Gandhi, *Ethical Religion* (Ganesan, Madras, 1922).

- M.K. Gandhi, *From Yeravda Mandir*, Tr. by V.G. Desai (Navajivan, Ahmedabad, 1932).

- M.K. Gandhi, *Hind Swaraj* (Navajivan, Ahmedabad, 1938).

- M.K. Gandhi, *Truth is God* (Ahmedabad, 1955).

- M.K. Gandhi, *All men are Brothers*, compiled and edited by K.Kripalani, UNESCO, 1958 & 1969.

- M.K. Gandhi, *In search of the Supreme*, Compiled by V.B. Kher, (Navajivan, Ahmedabad, 1931).

- *The Collected Works of Mahatma Gandhi* (Ahmedabad : Ministry of Information & Broadcasting, Govt. of India,1958) Vols. 1-70.

- *The Selected Works of Mahatma Gandhi*, edited by Sriman Narayan, Ahmedabad, 1968.

- *The Speeches and writings of Mahatma Gandhi* (Nateson, Madras), 1934.

- *Selections from Gandhi*, ed. by N.K. Bose (Navajivan, Ahmedabad, 1948).

- J.J. Doke, *M.K. Gandhi* (Nateson, 1909).

- L. Fischer (ed.), *The Essential Gandhi* (New York, 1962).
- Glyn Richards, *The Philosophy of Gandhi* (Curzon Press, London,1982).
- Raghavan N. Iyer, *The Moral and Political Thought of Mahatma Gandhi* (Oxford, 1978, Paperback).
- B.R. Nanda, *Mahatma Gandhi A Biography* (Allen & Unwin, 1958).
- C.F. Andrews, *Mahatma Gandhi's Ideas* (Allen & Unwin, 1949).
- D.G. Tendulkar and others (ed.) *Mahatma* (Ahmedabad, 1951.54).
- S. Ray (ed.), *Gandhi, India & World* (University of CaliforniaPress, 1970).
- Chandrashekhar (ed.) *Conversations of Gandhijee* (Bombay,1949).
- Diary of Mahadeva Desai (Navjivan, 1953).

B. Journals edited by Gandhi.

1. Harijan
2. Young India.

Other Works

- A. Coomarswami, *Buddha & the Gospel of Buddhism* (London, 1916).
- A.N. Whitehead, *Religion in the Making* (Macmillan, 1926).
- A.N. Whitehead, *Science and the Modern World* (Macmillan, 1926).

- Abernethy & Langford (ed.) *Philosophy of Religion* (Macmillan,1958).
- F. Schliermacher, *On Religion: Speeches to its Cultural Despisers* (Harper, New York, 1958).
- John Dewey, *A Common Faith* (Yale Univ. Press, New Haven,1934).
- P. Sitaramayya, *The History of the Indian National Congress* (Padma publications, 1946).
- Paul Tillich, *Systematic Theology* (University of Chicago, 1951).
- Paul Tillich, *Dynamics of Faith* (Harper, New York, 1958).
- Paul Tillich, *Christianity and the Encounter of the World Religion*(Columbia University Press, 1963).
- S. Radhakrishnan, *Eastern Religions and Western Thought* (Oxford. 1939).
- Jayaprakash Narayan, *Samājvāda, Sarvodaya Aur Lokatantra* (Bihar Hindi, Granth Akadami, Patna).
- A. Huxley, *Ends and Means* (London, 1941).
- A. Schweitzer, *Indian Thought and its Development*, 1936.
- *The Dhammapada* (Poona, Oriental Book Agency, 1939).
- *The Bhagvad-Gitā*.
- *Manusmriti* (Chowkhambā, 1979).
- *Koran* (All extracts taken from As. Arberry's The KoranInterprete (New York, 1955).
- *The Bible* (New Testament).
- *BrhdāranyakaUpnishada* (Chowkhambā, 1970).

❏